Endorsements

'A wonderful book, of great value to education. Every child deserves a school where the insights from this book are put into practice!'

René van Engelen, Director, Freinet Primary School

'This book creates scope for personal research and creation; cultural vitamins for children's brains.'

Felix Kreier PhD, Paediatrician and Brain Scientist

'The book is worth every penny! It gave me so many new starting points for thinking up lessons.'

Wiepkje Spoelstra, Artist Educator Language and Visual Arts

'This book is just one big plea for freedom. Working creatively without a predetermined plan – it is possible!'

Marijke Liefting, Co-Teacher Visual Arts

'You have to read this book. But more than that, you have to use it. It shows you how to shape children's own creative processes. No more predetermined handicraft projects or colouring books – children can create on their own!'

Millie Warradijn, Pedagogue Trainer and Studio Educator

'This book has great added value for children and everyone who interacts with children. I can take this inspiration to convince the people around me that it can be done differently, I am thrilled!'

Hildegarde Hooft, Director, Childcare Centre

'Learning through discovery is a core concept in this book. And rightly so! We can't discover anything that's already been demonstrated, while that which we have been able to discover for ourselves leads to lasting insights and skills.'

Ewald Vervaet PhD, Developmental Psychologist and Teacher

'I read this book from cover to cover during a long car journey. On arrival, I tried out the new knowledge I'd acquired; the children were immediately in supreme concentration.'

Maaike Ebbinge, Graphic Designer and Studio Educator

'A must-have book! You couldn't be any happier as a parent or a teacher.'

Veronique Vetjens, Remedial Educationalist

How Children Learn and Create Using Art, Play and Science

When children make beautiful drawings, we think it is wonderful. But many adults find it hard to understand what young children are doing when they scribble, smear, or draw endless lines, and why it is so difficult to motivate older children to draw or paint.

This book shows that creativity is so much more than drawing or painting something beautiful. It is a way of understanding the world through your hands and learning through art, play and science.

Drawing on the Reggio Emilia approach (among others), this book focuses on the process rather than the result and argues that children should be supported in experimenting with materials and mark-making. The authors go against traditional setups where an adult demonstrates how it should be done, showing instead that an inspiring environment and open-ended resources trigger children's intrinsic motivation. The book shows countless inexpensive possibilities, which require little preparation, and get children in a creative flow.

With its appealing full colour photographs, this fully updated English edition offers inspiration, a sustainable and feasible vision, and tools for facilitating creative processes at school, in childcare centres and at home. Full of practical guidance, it is essential reading for anyone working with children wanting to help them develop into self-aware, creative, and responsible people.

Sabine Plamper is a cultural pedagogue and photographer with many years of experience working with young children in studios. She was also the artist educator at a Reggio Emilia-inspired children's centre in Amsterdam. Since 2011, Sabine has been working with 18-month to 10-year-old children at her Kris Kras Studio and gives practical trainings for educators in the Netherlands and abroad.

Annet Weterings is an author of books and articles for childcare and primary school education. Her works include a Dutch book on experiencing nature: *Hear and see, smell, feel, taste*. She has also adapted four books by the British author Penny Tassoni on the theme of parenting and has written a guide on promoting reading for teachers and teaching assistants.

Cover Photo: © Sabine Plamper

First published in English 2024
by Routledge
4 Park Square, Milton Park, Abingdon, Oxon, OX14 4RN

and by Routledge
605 Third Avenue, New York, NY 10158

Routledge is an imprint of the Taylor & Francis Group, an informa business

© 2024 Sabine Plamper and Annet Weterings

The right of Sabine Plamper and Annet Weterings to be identified as authors
of this work has been asserted in accordance with sections 77 and 78 of the
Copyright, Designs and Patents Act 1988.

© Photography: Sabine Plamper

Except for the following photos:
Anja Booi (page 14, photo b, page 18, photo d)
Ohod Ahmad (page 14, photo h, page 16, IMG 2.15, photo b)
Elizabeth Venicz (IMG. 1.13)
Heidi de Geus (IMGs. 3.48 through 3.52 and page 160)
Ursula Woerner (IMGs. 1.15, 3.40, 3.41, IMG 3.61 photo b)
Jacqueline Koek (IMGs. 1.9, 3.34, 3.35)
Marie Christine Roeleveld (IMG. 3.62)
Mirja van der Bijl (IMGs. 3.55 through 3.57)
Anne van Paridon (IMG. 3.60)
Titia Sprey (IMG. 1.2, IMGs. 3.43 through 3.47 and page 156)
Rogier Alleblas (portrait Sabine Plamper, page 157)

First published in Dutch by Reed Business, Amsterdam 2012
Second edition, Bohn Stafleu van Loghum, Houten 2016
Third edition, Bohn Stafleu van Loghum, Houten 2019
Fourth, revised edition, Bohn Stafleu van Loghum, Houten 2021

Translation of the Dutch book: Lizzie Kean, Keanmachine
Editor: Anni McTavish, Early Years Creative Arts Consultant

British Library Cataloguing-in-Publication Data
A catalogue record for this book is available from the British Library

ISBN: 978-1-032-52382-8 (hbk)
ISBN: 978-1-032-52381-1 (pbk)

Typeset in Frutiger LT Std
by KnowledgeWorks Global Ltd.

Printed in the UK by Severn, Gloucester on responsibly sourced paper

How Children Learn and Create Using Art,
Play and Science

Understanding Through Your Hands

Sabine Plamper and Annet Weterings

Routledge
Taylor & Francis Group

LONDON AND NEW YORK

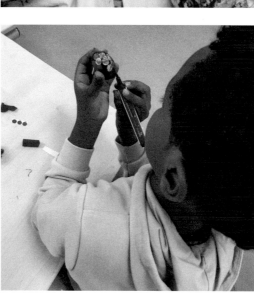

Preface

How Children Learn and Create Using Art, Play and Science: Understanding Through Your Hands makes a valuable contribution to early childhood delving into practices of mark-making, art and science, and learning though play. It has a balance of theory and practice, brought to life with strong illustrative images. Mark-making provides children with opportunities to follow their interests and make meaning. In doing so they express feelings and ideas, and develop theories of how the world works. Children discover understanding as they make sense of their experiences.

In the book the authors offer a way of working that places the child at the centre of their learning. Their work draws upon a rich heritage of thinkers within arts education, ideas which they have reworked and developed throughout the book, suggesting new contemporary ways of working.

This book looks at the important role of the educator in facilitating this journey, offering sensitive support and encouragement. It's about providing the conducive conditions: the space, time and resources for ideas to flourish. The authors highlight the importance of creating the environment for children to experiment, allowing them the freedom to immerse themselves in the process rather than the final output. They highlight that sensitive interaction takes many forms; it may be raising questions at the right moment, giving an acknowledging nod or offering encouragement to retain their interest and capture their creative flow.

Remaining open to possibilities and the unexpected is central, where the adult can also learn from the child. The authors highlight the importance of recognising and 'listening' to children's communication through their visual expression. They advocate taking a position of equivalence and being authentic in the way they interact, by viewing the child as capable and competent, thus respecting the child. Feeling valued, and having the freedom to be themselves in this way, builds self-esteem. As we make marks this outward expression builds a strong sense of agency.

This book also serves as a treasure chest of possibilities, with informed, low budget and sustainable suggestions for materials and resources. The delightful images of children working with materials in a rich variety of contexts included throughout the book provide inspiration. We can feel the children's energy, their curiosity and adventures of discovery. We can observe in the images, that children have had the freedom to find their voice and express their ideas. This approach will encourage intrinsic motivation and sustained concentration as children become deeply absorbed in their self-expression, which is evident in the examples. It is clear children are holistic learners, employing hands, heart and minds in the process, and with the visual arts, children take great delight in what their hands enable them to do.

The book contains plentiful practical advice, which has been gathered from many years working alongside

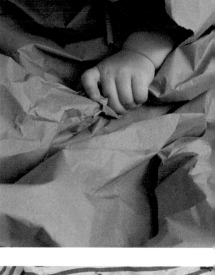

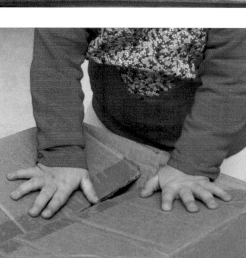
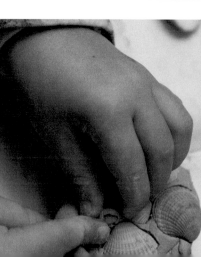

children and reflecting on practice. For instance they advise the 'crescendo', starting small, so both children and educators can gain confidence, therefore building on from what they know before introducing more complexity. The authors' ideas are further supported by examples of practitioners who have applied the way of working *Understanding Through Your Hands*.

This book was originally written in Dutch. It is a delight this book has now been translated into English to benefit a wider audience. The authors introduce thinkers that perhaps the English speaking audience are less familiar with such as Stern and Juul. This adds to the breadth that the book has to offer, as well as the inclusion of less familiar quotes from an array of educators.

The authors suggest finding your own style of the approach *Understanding Through Your Hands* and adapting it when necessary, but most importantly, they encourage you to enjoy those 'wow' moments of children's creative discoveries. Using our hands is experiential, it's learning through doing, active engagement, essentially about how children learn best. I think this book will inspire and perhaps allow us to reflect more deeply our own practice, and in turn, result in more children having positive experiences and flourishing along the journey.

Pete Moorhouse
Fellow of the Royal Society of Arts
Churchill Fellow
Early Childhood Creative Consultant, Bristol, UK

Contents

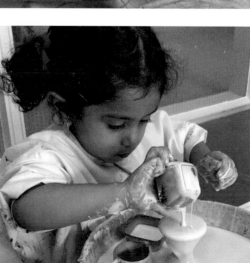

Introduction

How Children Learn and Create Using Art, Play and Science: Understanding Through Your Hands aims to pass on inspiring notions about children and creativity to parents and professional educators, for example, for all those who work with children in a school, in a childcare centre or in a museum. For us, it's abundantly clear that the old, frequently seen ideas about teaching creative activities are in need of a review. In this book, rather than focusing on making a beautiful or artistic product, or even on the term 'creativity', we simply look at the *marks* children make. Then, play, art and science come together.

How can we adults make it possible for children to learn and create of their own accord? How can we support them to feel inspired? We need to give children the space to learn through self-discovery, using all of their senses. This can take place in a number of disciplines, for example, through drawing, painting, dance, music, technology, philosophy, drama or through experiencing nature. Rather than directing, we want to motivate, facilitate and support; allowing children to discover, formulate and express their own image of the world, instead of having any adult-perceived ideas forced upon them.

We wrote this book to be an inspiring basic guide to a sustainable and feasible vision on creative learning. It focuses on the attitudes, the materials and tools that you, the adult, can use when facilitating children's creative activities. Everyone can adopt the approach *Understanding Through Your Hands*. It does, however, require you to be aware of a several important principles. They are neither complex nor expensive. All that is needed is courage, and a willingness to let go of old values and immerse yourself in new ones.

The most important principle of our way of working is equivalence between adults and children. Then comes the regular practice of working without predetermined examples, and avoiding inflexible themes or assignments. If these principles are applied, you will see motivated children who are able to concentrate and enjoy their playing and learning, with adults who are enjoying co-discovering.

Facilitating creative activities according to the *Understanding Through Your Hands* approach is not without obligations. Showing restraint does not mean that you are lounging around, or inattentive. It takes effort to facilitate children skilfully, and interact at just the right moment, whether that's with a nod, a pen or a single word. It takes a certain mindset, knowledge, experience and the willingness to discover the world alongside the child. This can be learned by trial and error: offering structure and setting boundaries are also part of the process. As is a bit of creative chaos. You would not want to hold a child back who is in the flow, but you would want to avoid *destructive* chaos.

Art education and the importance of creative learning are hot topics in our society. We wish to underline the importance of art education in a way that also leaves scope for the child's input. We want children to have

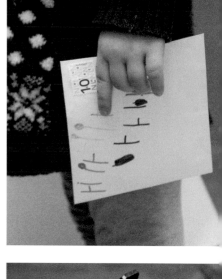
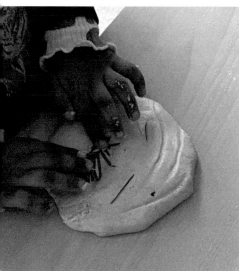

the space, time and materials with which to develop individually, in their own way and at their own pace. Our vision is based on the philosophies of Jesper Juul, Arno Stern and the educators of Reggio Emilia, and has been developed through practice to become the *Understanding Through Your Hands* way of working. So it combines old and new accomplishments.

In preparation for writing this book, we visited and spoke to artists, educators, subject teachers and the boards of educational institutes both in the Netherlands and Germany. Everywhere we went, we saw people facing a centuries-old dilemma: how to find the right balance between wanting to teach a child something, and wanting to give them the space to shape their own world. There was pride and frustration regarding time restrictions, funding and alternative possibilities. Nowhere was it perfect. The similarities in theoretical principles are striking. We have incorporated them into our way of working, and structured them to be practical tools, necessary for facilitating the creative process and maintaining it.

Although we would love to integrate music, dance and drama with the visual arts, we will restrict ourselves in this book to the latter. Firstly, this allows us to focus on them specifically, and secondly, because they are within our own professional field and the ones where we feel most at home. In addition, practitioners get a wonderful instrument to use, with all the materials listed and displayed in this book. An instrument with which children can make marks and discover and learn of their own accord.

In the past ten years, this approach of *Understanding Through Your Hands* has found its way into many studios, schools, childcare centres and kitchen tables in the Netherlands and Belgium. We are very happy that the book has been translated into English, in order that more people can become familiar with the philosophy and the practice. Let the book inspire you, expect the unexpected and let the children's creative discoveries delight and amaze you!

Sabine Plamper, Cultural Pedagogue and Photographer
Annet Weterings, Pedagogue
Titia Sprey, Visual Artist/Studio Educator, Atelier in een Koffer

2023

1 Investigating is experiencing, learning – it's creativity

1.1 The importance of making your own marks

Adults often have expectations when children are making something: 'What's it going to be?' But children are more interested in how things work. An interest in how things work is crucial to learning; only then are children intrinsically motivated and this is when they learn best.

Learning is a process. It involves being happily occupied – investigating and experimenting, with neither adults or children envisaging a pre-determined end result.

Children leave their marks everywhere
Children leave their marks while playing. If adults 'read' these marks correctly, they will see what children are searching for, what they marvel at, and what surprises them.

IMG. 1.1   When taking off shoes, sand falls on the parquet. The boy spontaneously draws in the sand.
<
IMG. 1.2   Fascinated, making marks in the sand with a stick and watching what happens.

Marks often occur intuitively. Children are generally unaware that they are making marks. As an adult, you don't only see the marks; you also hear the children's questions, their remarks and the sounds which accompany them. These are clues that enable us to help the children to take the next step. Once a child is underway, one mark leads to another. Put a small amount of flour on the table and children will do all kinds of things with it: scoop, spread and feel. Unprompted, stories about snow or polar bears will come. A box of bottle tops leads to counting, or making a sound (jingling inside a cardboard box) and perhaps to a trail of 'cars', or a 'traffic queue'.

> If you get one idea, you get more and more ideas!
> Cas, aged 5

What happens if I do this?
Making their *own* marks precedes looking at and understanding what others are making. Pencil scribbles on a piece of paper are marks that occur both consciously and unconsciously. There comes a moment when the child realises that they, and no-one else, are the person making those marks. It is important that they get the chance to make their *own* marks: *I* made that line on the paper. And by scribbling over it or smearing paint on it, *I* can make it disappear. I draw; therefore I am! Babies do this by making marks in yoghurt with their fingers, or by drawing a line with their finger in the sand. The combination of consciously and unconsciously making marks leads to personal discoveries, 'wow' moments, and children learn a lot from those. Coincidence also generally plays a major role.

Focus on the process, not on the result

Children look at themselves in that process. They reflect on what they do, as it were, and add the experience to their previous ones. You might say that children observe themselves as they are making marks.

1.2 Materials research in order to understand the world

Experimenting and gaining experience
Materials research is one way of understanding the world. By experimenting, children gain new experiences that they add to their learning process. If they have to deliver a product that has to look like whatever an adult pictures, that process is blocked. There is no longer any experimentation. Children must be given the opportunity to investigate in their own way, at their own pace.

IMG. 1.3   While washing his hands, a boy grasps the cardboard cylinder of an empty toilet roll and watches how
<   water flows through it. The cylinder becomes wet, so it tears easily. The child takes another cardboard cylinder to make it wet, and carefully takes it apart until he has a flat piece of cardboard. In the end, he has papier mâché. One mark leads to another.

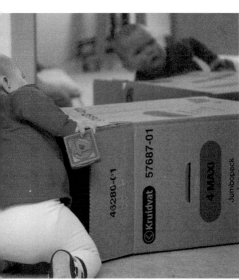

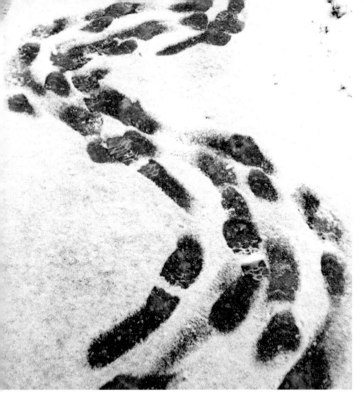

IMG. 1.5   Fresh snow invites an awareness of making marks.

Materials research contributes to children's development because it is intriguing, tangible and inviting. It is fantastic for sharpening observation: what does the material do? The colour, the shape, how does it feel? Does it behave compliantly, does it resist? Does it change? Children learn by trying things out, by making marks. Materials research results in the first unexpected mark and one thing leads to another. During this process, children don't think about whether something is right or wrong, it just *is*. Young children, in particular, have no fear that something might fail.

IMG. 1.4   24 verbs describe what this baby does with boxes: hide, wear, push, put it on their head, turn it upside
<   down, build, stack, climb, slide, turn, bite it, make a step-up, jump, crawl on hands and knees (through
         the tunnel), hit, throw, hammer on it, rattle it, put things in it, tear it, put several in a line and use it as a
         tunnel, fall on it, and through it. Terms that the educator uses in conversation with the child: big/small,
         high/low, broken/whole, open/shut, now/later, away/back.

25

IMG. 1.7   Corn or potato starch is a fascinating non-Newtonian material, because, mixed with a little water, it turns from liquid to solid when pressure is applied. Children investigate this rubbery consistency in great detail.

Are marks beautiful?

To be honest, the concept 'beautiful' does not really matter. 'Beautiful' is a strange notion. Are doodles and scribbled drawings 'beautiful'? Is everything children make actually 'beautiful'? The word reflects your own standards and values and is therefore always subjective. And that is exactly the problem. Because adults are always wanting to stimulate children positively, they're quick to say that something's beautiful. It's a pity, and not even true. The fact is, that when you call everything that children make 'beautiful', you make them dependent on your judgement. Does a child still find what they are doing worthwhile, if you forget to say it's beautiful sometimes? Not only that, but constantly crying out 'beautiful' generates rivalry between children; why does she like the drawing made by the girl next to me, and not mine?

Be careful with 'beautiful'!

When two fathers worked creatively in our studio, the conversations was also about 'beautiful'. One father said: 'Do you think what I'm making is beautiful?' The other father asked: 'And mine, is mine beautiful too?' 'What is it really about?' I answered, 'Surely not whether it's beautiful or not? Isn't it more about how you are working here?'
Tihana Trputec, Altijd Lente Children's Centre, Amsterdam

IMG. 1.6   Children are busy discovering, not making something beautiful. After a long session painting
<   on paper, the paint board itself is inviting: feel it and make marks.

IMG. 1.8   A child discovers that they can use the caps as scoops. They throw the rice from one cap to the other and onto the paper. There's a big 'mess' but the child is actually working very meticulously.

Being allowed to make a mess

By making a mess, children experience what a material does. And while they're doing that, they are observing themselves too: what do I think of this? Do I like it or shall I try something different? When adults are making or repairing something, they also make a mess. It's the same with children. Playing simply involves mess and risks. Adults sometimes choose safe alternatives that mean children are always clean, quiet, accurate and orderly at play, but this means children don't get the chance to daub and mess around, to scribble and muddle along, to smear and take apart, to try out and choose, to enjoy and experience – in short, to discover.

> I'm going to make some lovely mud!
> Amin, aged 3

Children are often obliged by their parents to stay tidy. Getting their expensive clothes dirty is not an option.
Lenka Slivkova, Altijd Lente Children's Centre, Amsterdam

1.3   Making marks and learning through discovery

Working without a theme

At home, with parents or nannies, in childcare centres and schools and even in arts centres, children are often, with the best of intentions, given themes to work with. But the more children have to carry out compulsory assignments, the less time there is for spontaneous activities. Leaving plenty of room for freedom of choice means responding to children's individuality. We advocate letting children draw, paint and investigate as much as possible without themes, examples or a programme. Instead, we suggest offering interesting and suitable material that triggers mark-making and investigation. That way, children can stay close to themselves, thus giving their uniqueness a chance to express itself from the subconscious.

Children don't need ideas thought up by an adult.

IMG. 1.10   Young children want to see for themselves what they can do with a felt-tipped pen, on a small and a large scale. It is about children following their own marks and observing themselves. Assignments and examples are not in line with this.

> The conscious self is a channel, as it were, for that which your subconscious comes up with. Both the arts and science rely on inspiration. That's another word for your subconscious being productive.
> Dijksterhuis 2012

Children are filled with impressions from their own busy lives. The great danger of following programmes is that it can be easy to lose sight of children's needs and interests. Therefore, it is essential to regularly offer children creative activities that have no theme. This does not mean that the children no longer have a context or a footing from which to begin, for it is the material that forms the starting point, not the theme. The material offers a framework and connections with the real world. It is also possible to make a link to a theme through your *choice* of materials. Most importantly, the end result must not be fixed.

> Painting spontaneously, without a theme, is a lifelong source of creativity and independence. Drawing something in the sand with a stick and scribbling on paper means being in touch with yourself. And it's not about communication or aesthetics, or even about a message; the marks children make are not intended for anyone in particular.
> Stern 2008

IMG. 1.9   This child is drawing lines on a small piece of paper with various felt-tipped pens. They are making marks
<   without a predefined theme and are engrossed in the activity.

IMG. 1.12   What does wallpaper paste feel like? Nice or nasty?

Children, allowed to examine things freely and discover, reinforce their inner cornerstone, their belief in themselves. With that kind of motivation, coming from the inside, you already have the first spark. And that spark provides a good foundation on which to build learning processes.
Vecchi 2010

IMG. 1.11   Five children are standing behind the table. One of them sticks her brush into the paste pot, holds it up
< and looks at it, fascinated. The good-sized blob of paste is slowly turning into something resembling an icicle. 'Hey, a drip,' she says. Her neighbour says: 'I'm going to drip too.' 'It's even longer now!' the first child says. She looks on in amazement as the drip slowly gets longer and longer and finally falls off the brush. It is up to us to see where children's interests lie; we have to respond to them. This morning, our children were talking about storms, snow and hailstones. When they came in, someone was making a 'thunderstorm'. You go along with that: what is a thunderstorm, how does it feel? What does it look like? I then look for materials to use: what is soft? What does snow make you think of? I had glue, paper and pieces of polystyrene. I don't say anything, I just offer the materials and watch. Now, raindrops come out. I ask more questions about that. Here they are allowed to play with the glue, to find out how it feels. Glue is not meant just for gluing, you can do other things with it too, like letting drops of glue fall. That feeling, experiencing … that's what it's about! (Claudia Zinnemers, Uit de Kunst Children's Centre, Amersfoort).

Amazement and questions

To work regularly without a theme is new for some people. The idea often generates disbelief, amazement or questions. Children and creativity are regularly associated with handicrafts, colouring books, predetermined cutting-out or an easy craft example from the Internet. Since the examples come from adults, a child's imagination and the development of their own visual language have little chance of being expressed. Examples from adults often show little creativity. Adults may have more experience and skill than children, but at the same time, they are frequently perfectionist and rational. And because they want to help children, they demonstrate things. Adults generally work in a targeted way according to realistic drawing or handicrafts. The result is that children feel they are being lectured. If children are forced to meet the expectations and realistic images of the world as presented by the adults, the result is either dissatisfying – because the likeness is not good, or not good-enough – or it is the same for every child, so all the pieces look identical.

Being allowed to scribble is valuable for all age groups

Often, children either have *no* finished product in mind, or it can change along the way because, by examining the material, they associate from one discovery to the next. They learn what they *want* to learn and not what they *have* to learn. They take all the time they need, repeating or redoing, all the while making mistakes and correcting themselves.

> 'Scribbling is art,' says 5-year-old Lara to her friend Mare. And both children go on to enthusiastically scribble page after page. Is scribbling right for a 5-year-old? The answer is 'Yes!'. Scribbling is right for all age groups and in particular, for primary school children. It is essential for using up energy, coming up with an idea, 'warming up' and for not feeling any pressure to make something beautiful. Even adults happily draw subconscious scribbles, while on the phone, for example, or during a meeting: it's called *doodling*. Doodles have no predetermined meaning, just like children's scribbled drawings.
> Plamper, 2011

Learning by experiencing

There is not really that much difference between how children learn and how adults learn. Both learn best through experiencing, by personally trying things out, or 'learning through doing'. The resulting reflection – 'How do I feel about this?', 'Have I experienced this before?' – follows automatically because we are intrigued by something. Experiences are where learning begins.

IMG. 1.13 Children discover things with the simplest of materials: a pound of flour in a baking tin, for example.
< This boy makes his fingerprints disappear by pressing a second baking tin onto the first. To his amazement, he sees how smooth the surface of the flour has become. He then makes a new imprint and repeats the actions several times. Foodstuffs like flour, rice or lentils are perfectly suitable materials for young children. Safe and interesting! It is sustainable when using expired foodstuffs and when reusing the material endless times. In that way many children gain from this type of multi-sensory play.

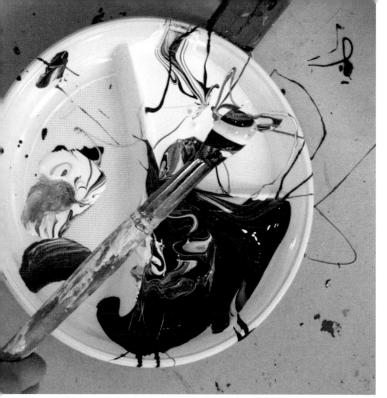

IMG. 1.15   This girl first brushes black and white paint onto the paper. Later, she dips her hand in the paint to feel it.

Children who experience things by feeling, looking, listening, tasting and smelling, will focus on everything that happens near them. If they are allowed to do this in their own way, and at their own pace, you can *see* them becoming enthusiastic. They continue to discover new properties of the materials: big/small, light/heavy, fine/rough, exciting/calming … and it is thrilling every single time. Experiencing and self-esteem are connected; a child's self-esteem increases with the smallest of things they have made themselves: 'Wow! I made that myself!' Bamford 2006

As an adult, the skill is to take a good look at *how* children experience: how do they respond to what you say to them? What are their facial expressions, their body language? What do they say? To you, or to each other? That is how you notice what appeals to them and what does not.

The importance of concentration and tranquillity

Discovery-based learning and concentration go together. The assumption that young children cannot concentrate is incorrect. Give a child the right material and don't disturb them, but facilitate with attention, and you will

IMG. 1.14   The children are regularly given the opportunity to draw. They are occupied for around an hour,
<   concentrating on drawing stories and, in between times, scribbling spontaneously and energetically.

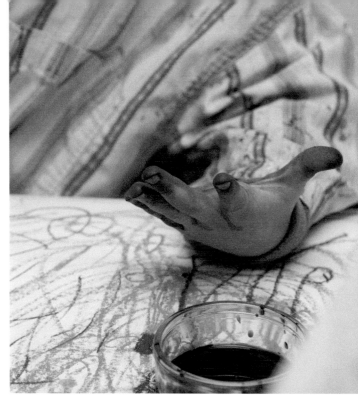

IMG. 1.18   The 'wow' moment. In her book *The Wow Factor*, Anne Bamford, an Australian educator and professor, writes about children's 'wow' moments: those are magical moments in which they come across something surprising, to their own amazement – wow! 'Wow' means there is excitement, a fun discovery, a surprise. Moments like this often indicate a turning point, an instance which leads children to undertake something new. As an educator, you can use 'wow' to replace 'beautiful'. The word 'beautiful' expresses an opinion in terms of beautiful or ugly. But by saying 'wow', you are not making a judgement, you are sharing in the children's enthusiasm and their experience.

see an 18-month-old meticulously cutting small pieces from a piece of paper or painting for a whole hour.

> Concentration is the polarisation of attention.
> Maria Montessori

A child who feels they are being challenged by something that evokes both pleasure and wonder will make one mark after the other. Intrinsically motivated, they will become fully engrossed in what they are doing.

In such moments, they are in 'flow', and forget about the world around them. This happens during long and intensive periods of concentration. Once in flow, children make new discoveries; for example, they might suddenly see a tree in a line or an elephant in a drip. These are 'wow' moments.

> Reading, writing and maths should always be in service of wonder.
> Jelle Jolles

IMG. 1.16   From dry to wet: first, the child feels the soft, dry, crackly cornflour. Later, water is added and they
<<   examine how the material feels now.

IMG. 1.17   Whereas other children dislike getting their hands dirty, this boy squeezes the sponge full of
<   watercolour with both hands. He is concentrating and discovering what effect the watercolour
           has on his hands and on the paper.

IMG. 1.19 Adults sometimes assume that drawing or painting is relaxation, in a similar way to 'having a chat'. But there must be peace and quiet if you are to be able to concentrate. Consider what it is like for you: you also need a little peace and quiet in order to be able to fully relax. No distractions. This kind of silent attention is important for children, too. An intense focus, watching without words and without judgement of what they're making often leads to children sharing what is going on in their minds.

Sometimes, speech is silver and silence is golden.

Adults will enjoy the moments when a child displays enthusiasm and is deeply involved. The American-Hungarian psychologist, Mihaly Csikszentmyhályi, put forward the idea of 'flow' to describe the process of being fully engaged in an experience. He believed that the state of being in 'flow', was 'the optimum situation for being able to learn' (Csikszentmyhályi 2008).

1.4   A process of shaping is a process of developing awareness

To each child their own reality
Children name what they experience and make connections between different experiences. These connections lead to forming their own thoughts. This is how they build their knowledge of the world. In the same way as adults, what and how a child observes varies from one child to another. This is why it is not about whether your child's reality is your reality. It is about a child being allowed to develop their own reasoning and thinking about how the world works.

Children who start with a line, drawn on paper with a pen or pencil, work more neatly than children who start from a blob (clay, ink, mud, or paint). Both ways of working lead to associations and discoveries, but adults often experience drips and smudges as dirty or careless. This is a pity, because being allowed to make a mess (just a bit) is part of the creative process. Children build understanding through their hands. They develop their ideas from these experiences.

IMG. 1.20   While painting, this boy discovers that you can mix paint and flour together. He is not just making a mess; he is learning in his own way how blobs behave if you mix them with various materials.

In order to sharpen a child's observation skills, it's important to show them the real world, in all its diversity. Children are fantastic at observing details. With children, you discover that we live in a world brim-full of remarkable and exciting things. If we take the time to notice and participate, we see that children have a watchful eye on everything. A worthwhile vision for us as adults too.

Process of shaping leads to accumulation of knowledge
Experience → observe → become aware → name → connect → thoughts → accumulation of knowledge

IMG. 1.21 and 1.22 >, >>   The girl is making a lump of clay into a flat surface. She draws on it and cuts into it. At a certain moment, a figure is created separate from the flat surface. She supports the figure with long arms. She develops this herself, without saying anything.

IMG. 1.26   An 18-month-old girl is painting and after a while, calls out 'car'. This is an example of a 'wow' moment and a process of developing awareness: the child associates the roller turning with the wheels of a car. She observes a vital component of the car as a symbol – the wheel.

IMG. 1.23
<<<   The boy is covering his fingers with the paint and suddenly starts to count: 'One, two, three, four, five, six, seven. And eight, and nine, and ten.' The attending adult asks: 'How many fingers are you using now?' The child answers: 'One, two …' (counts to eleven) and says: 'You have to do it with your hands too!' The boy places his fingers against those of the attending adult and counts all ten of *her* fingers.

IMG. 1.24
<<   This boy is examining material in his own way. First, he wants to make clay worms with the garlic press, as he did last time. Then he draws and hammers on the clay. He makes a hole in the clay with his finger and pours water into it. He really enjoys the sploshing sound and the feeling he gets from pushing his finger into the hole. He keeps calling out: 'I've made a fountain!'

IMG. 1.25
<   In order to educate children without judgement, I neither praise them nor criticise them. We don't work according to a theme or subject; children are led by their inner images. They decide what happens. Often, a lump of clay will first be turned into a flat surface that is then examined with the hands, fingers or with tools. It is perforated, beaten and given a structure.
(Silke Ratzeburg, Kindergarten Kinderland, Berlin).

IMG. 1.27
>   Creativity does not mean that a child makes something completely new, rather, that they may come across something while playing, and in doing so, discover something new and different to them. It can have a lot to do with coincidence, for example, the cause is often ordinary but the effect may be astonishment and joy. It ensues from something you do intensively and with pleasure. This boy helps with making soup at home. He gets in flow with shaping and arranging the vegetables. While eating the soup later on, he tries to find the shapes he made earlier and the play continues.

IMG. 1.28   This boy is looking attentively at a wooden doll and suddenly says: 'It doesn't have any eyes'. The studio educator asks him if he would like a felt-tipped pen to draw some eyes on. He nods, and draws eyes on lots of dolls, and places them on the cardboard he's been gluing things on.

Creativity is really everyday

Mark-making, shaping processes and creativity are close neighbours. For those who, at the mention of creativity, think of art – art is a charged notion. Some adults think of 'art' as something distant because they associate it with expensive paintings and art galleries. Letting children consciously experience through the senses is about expanding their knowledge of the world, not about turning them into little artists. It's about ordinary, everyday creativity and play, gaining experiences and learning through art. Sometimes there are results, sometimes there are not. This is still worthwhile and puts the focus firmly on the process.

Lastly: learning from marks made

By playing and making their own marks, children are able to make their own discoveries; 'wow' moments. At such times, a shaping process shifts to a process of developing awareness; as children quite literally are building their understanding through their hands. The things that children explore of their own volition are in line with their interests, and are always at their own level of development. All these experiences contribute to the child's developing brain and to their well-being. That is why play is the optimum form of learning.

2 Visions on guiding creative processes

2.1 Educational and creative sources of inspiration

Your attitude towards children determines how you treat them. Your expectations of what they can and cannot do will determine how they behave. It determines how you talk to them, what you say and when and how you intervene. If you assume that children are 'empty vessels' and must learn everything from you, then they will behave differently, as opposed to the assumption that, in principle, they have every capacity to be capable learners, and are able to discover for *themselves*.

A vision on how you develop such an open attitude does not appear out of thin air; it is formed. It is formed by

IMG. 2.1 Drawings are being made on a large strip of wrapping paper, which is also being used to make a house. Showing restraint as an educator does not mean that you are just adopting a wait-and-see approach; rather, you act with intention to create the right atmosphere; for example, this may involve providing materials in order to induce play.

your upbringing, your experiences and your passions. We, the authors, became inspired, all the while experimenting, observing, reading, talking, working, travelling and discussing, by our own experiences but even more so by those of others: initially by those of Jesper Juul, Arno Stern and the educators of Reggio Emilia. Our ideas were later also augmented by words and images of the studio educators we visited on location.

2.1.1 Jesper Juul

The Danish family therapist, Jesper Juul, sets great store by the creation of self-esteem in a child, and the indication and acknowledgement of personal boundaries in adults and children.

Self-esteem is not the same as self-confidence, which is derived from your accomplishments. Self-esteem is to do with how you think about yourself. A child with high self-esteem is contented, and usually good at dealing with setbacks. In particular, Juul emphasises the interactions between adults and children, including the dilemma of choosing between an authoritarian approach, and one in which children take part in the decision making. To Juul, accepting a child as they are

IMG. 2.2   Jenthe Baeyens (left) joins a boy in her class in looking at his work. She does not speak of it being beautiful or ugly, instead, she talks about how he has made this, and what his thought process was. Nicole Roel (right) asks if anyone needs more papier mâché. The children come to her and carry the full board back to the table. Both educators behave towards the children with respect and take them seriously.

is treating them as an equivalent, which is different from the idea of letting a child join in decisions about everything. Listening to a child does not immediately mean that you are negotiating, merely that you value them, and their right to their opinion and their ideas.

Discovery-based learning and the basis: a strong sense of self-esteem

A creative process begins with an open, exploratory attitude. This requires a sense of security and freedom. You have to be allowed to discover the world yourself. It is the responsibility of the adults to create an environment which allows and makes this possible. It can be a precarious process. Children's responses may differ; for example, they may say: 'I don't like that at all' or they may sometimes be altogether too inclined to go along with the directions given by the adults. The adults must find the right balance between offering materials and suggestions, and, going along with whatever it is that the children contribute.

Children with a good sense of self-esteem respond openly and freely. Low self-esteem can result in insecurity and self-criticism. Jesper Juul believes that children develop self-esteem when adults trust them and accept them as they are.

Being authentic

An authentic attitude is paramount for learning through discovery. By authentic, we mean that you avoid playing a role; for example, you do not assume a stereotype that you think is right for adults who supervise children. Children need to be approached with respect, and given responsibility. When responding to children who are searching for boundaries, it is important to develop your personal authority. Steer clear of accusations, criticisms or disappointment in your voice. Dare to be

yourself, be real, and consider your personal boundaries carefully: where are they exactly?

Equivalence and learning from each other

Genuine interest means that you, as an adult, take your place *next* to the child, and are open to learning from them. This is not always self-evident in a culture where genuine interests and emotions are sometimes suppressed by the pressures of time and workload. If you succeed in taking a position of authentic equivalence, you will learn from each other.

Equivalence versus equality

Taking a position of equivalence does not mean that adults and children are *equal*. Adults have more experience and a more formed overview. You have to, and want to, pass on that experience. You do that by making choices on behalf of children. For example, which of the children's ideas do you pick up on and encourage them to explore? What materials do you choose? Where do you go and sit? How do you make sure there is peace, and space, and that materials are tidied away? What questions do you ask, to whom and how? This is supported by a clear set of beliefs and rules. Though not any less valuable, children often have different attitudes to adults, and can be: associative, spontaneous, and inquisitive.

Personal boundaries

Equivalence does not mean that all things are allowed and that the children are in charge. On the contrary, it's important to give children clarity – and consequently security – by keeping a close watch on your own boundaries, without overstepping the children's. Juul believes that every individual should set clear personal boundaries, to aid clarity and avoid confusion. Adults are presumed to be able to do that; children are still

IMG. 2.3   Boundaries around the child

The adult's personal boundaries

learning how to. This is why it is necessary for the adult to treat the child's personal boundaries with respect, even during conflict situations (left half of IMG.2.3, the circle around the child).

Conversely, the adult must indicate *their* personal boundary appropriately (right half of IMG. 2.3, the semicircle around the adult). That way, the child learns how to respect others. Wording your boundary in the first person, for example: 'I don't like it when you shout like that, it disturbs me,' the more likely the child will understand and respond. Impersonal or unspecific boundaries mean nothing to a child.

Jesper Juul and the creative process
For us, equivalence is the basis of the creative process: there is so much that adults can learn from children, and children need adults because they have experience and knowledge of materials, and are in charge of organising and presenting these.

If both adults and children are involved in discovery and research, the result is an active exchange. This is how children develop their sense of self. This relationship allows both adults and children to better understand each other and the world. When adults take the experiences and questions of children seriously, children express and visualise their journey of discovery in their own unique way. Baeyens 2011

2.1.2   Arno Stern

His vision
Arno Stern developed his vision about the autonomy of children who paint, based on his professional practice. He devised a painting studio in Paris after World War II, whereby children and adults could come to paint each week. He has enthused followers all over the world.

IMG. 2.4a   The development of the circle based on the primal scribble

Stern's key aim was to make sure that children can paint, unconcerned by themes. He says: 'Children have a natural, rich source of ideas. Give them the peace and space to develop, and they achieve their own images. You paint for yourself, not for others. Only in this way can you develop your own visual language, which frequently results in unconscious elements emerging into the conscious.' Stern believes that adults, particularly where drawing and painting is concerned, too often aim for a quick fix in learning or direction. He gives children the confidence that they can do it themselves.

One of the important points in Stern's vision is his ideas about basic shapes. According to Stern, these basic shapes can be found all around us: the circle, the dot, the line, the spiral, the arch, the triangle, the rectangle, the square and the cross. Rather than forcing ready-made adult images on to children, they will discover these basic shapes for themselves. They will recognise these in everyday objects, and use them to express everything they want to.

In Stern's studio, adults and children paint next to each other in equivalence. They work on painting walls, with one communal palette in the middle of the studio. Once finished, the paintings disappear into his archives so that they would not be exposed to criticism or judgement. This idea stems from working without judgement – the aim of which is to create a calming effect for the makers, so that

IMG. 2.4b   The basic shapes of visual language

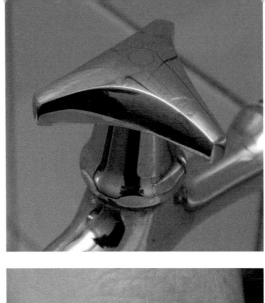

they can express themselves freely. Our vision coincides with this way of working – free of themes and judgement, and in the belief that conscious and unconscious processes are simultaneously involved in the creative process.

The effect of rules

Arno Stern has a clear goal in mind with his rules: to create tranquillity and a relaxed ambience. From there, it is possible to create – this is how children discover the basic shapes. Opponents of Arno Stern's way of working find his rules too rigid, but in practice, these rules ultimately ensure that the children feel safe and free to express themselves.

Arno Stern's painting studios in schools

Painting studios, inspired by Arno Stern's approach, have been set up in a number of schools and after-school childcare centres in Germany and Switzerland. The German book *Sehreise* by *Elisabeth* Walder and Beatrice Zschokke (2008) describes how this type of painting studio can be incorporated into the teaching programme. Thanks to its clear and simple format, it is possible to appeal to both boisterous and reserved children and invite them to the 'Play-of-Painting'. The book also recommends the benefits of this type of studio for children who are bi- or mono-lingual, or are yet to develop language. Painting is a universal language, and will therefore contribute to all children's development and well-being. These experiences will offer children space and many possibilities for expressing themselves. Initially, a gym class was scheduled after a painting hour because it was thought that children would need the extra exercise. However, the painting resulted in the children becoming focused and quiet, so a maths lesson was scheduled instead. It was also interesting to note that following these non-judgemental painting sessions, there was a better atmosphere in the class and fewer conflicts.

Older children and working without a theme

Working freely, without a theme, is also worthwhile for older children. It might seem too unrestricted, but the objective is to take children and their ideas seriously, which will help to promote their intrinsic motivation. Pupils often tell teachers who regularly offer open and free-choice lessons, that these are their favourites. It is important that there is a well-considered selection of materials that at the same time offer a context (for example, wood and wood glue or clay with stones and sticks). It is precisely these restrictions that provide direction, and make it feasible within a classroom situation for children to come up with their own, sometimes surprising ideas. In a similar way, there must be sufficient scope for materials research, and no predetermined end result.

Folkert Haanstra, former lecturer in arts and culture education, advocates for 'authentic arts education', in secondary schools too. He believes that arts education is intended to teach children to think up their own solutions and to shape whatever drives them. He would like to see art in schools being taught more in line with the pupils' own world, and children being

IMG. 2.5   Basic shapes are all around us.

<   Top left to right: apple = circle with dot in the middle, tap = triangle, spokes = sun symbol
Middle left to right: street furniture = triangle, ring = spiral, sponge = rectangle
Bottom left to right: desk confetti = little circles, drain = big circle with small circles inside,
piano keys = lines

involved in more complex issues that they initiate, rather than ready-made assignments. Haanstra wants to send children off to explore for themselves, to let them work things out, in order to offer them autonomy and independence. And he would have artists make assessments of what the children do, rather than the school. This requires collaboration between artists and teachers who believe in the value of pupils setting their own assignments and searching for their own solutions. Experiencing, and doing things independently is the priority; whereas transferring knowledge comes in second place.

That is not to say that the teacher leaves everything to the pupils; it takes a lot of organising and good supervision. Things are the other way round in primary education where teaching art is often very uncommitted: 'As long as they're having fun.' That's not what you want; it's about a happy medium.
Interview, *Cultuurplein Magazine*,
(December 2011), no. 2, Page 9

The role of the conscious and the unconscious in creative processes

The conscious is much revered in our western way of thinking. While, in fact, it is the unconscious that drives our behaviour, our thinking, and our feelings, and has a greater capacity for processing (Dijksterhuis 2012). When working with themes and product-oriented assignments, it is mainly children's conscious thought that is being triggered. The unconscious is also doing its work, but in general, we do not pay so much attention to it.

Unconscious thought is crucial to creativity. Some psychologists call it *incubation time*. Einstein, too, came to this conclusion: he visualised solutions first without being able to express them in words. When you have a question, you first consciously look up the necessary information with regard to the question, but the unconscious comes up with the solution – this is the creative thought. Only later, when the associations you

IMG. 2.6 Andrea Flach of Villa Comenius in Berlin adheres to Arno Stern's way of working.
< She says: 'The rules in Arno Stern painting studios are very clear. You repeat them a number of times until the children have absorbed them. There are rules about social interaction and rules about how you treat the material. For example, children do not comment on each other's work, or compare their work in the sense of better or worse, and neither do the adults. The following are the rules about the material:
– you stand directly in front of the paint pot with your brush
– first, you dip your brush in the water, and take off any excess on the rim of the jar, then you dip it in the paint
– you do not splash the paint around
– you will be given a piece of paper measuring 50 x 70 cm (19 ¾ x 27 ½ inch)
– the attending adult will fix it to the wall with drawing pins
– the attending adult will give you a step to stand on if you wish to paint higher up
– the attending adult will collect the brushes when you are finished painting.

IMG. 2.7 This girl is concentrating on painting an animal and brown stripes. She then makes the painting 'grow'
> by continuing to paint on an adjoining piece of paper. The three brown stripes become trees. Later, she does a new painting. Meanwhile, the first one, in two parts, is drying at the top of the painting wall.

have collected while playing have settled sufficiently, do you search for the words to go with the solution. The conscious thinking process is necessary afterwards in order to be able to explain it to other people. Dijksterhuis 2012

In Arno Stern's theme-free way of working, the unconscious is given multiple opportunities. It plays a greater part in the process. The result is that children have the freedom to begin to explore visually, from the unconscious to the conscious. Their mark-making often leads them to their personal visual theme, and gives the painting process scope, without the need for a focus on the end product.

2.1.3 Reggio Emilia and working structurally through research

Children are competent researchers

Reggio Emilia is a small town in Northern Italy. After World War II, and under the enthusiastic supervision of the educator and philosopher Loris Malaguzzi (1920–1994), parents started setting up nursery schools and children's centres that broke with the pedagogical and educational traditions of the time. The basis of the Reggio Emilia philosophy is that young children have every potential in them from birth and are focused on communication. They do not only express themselves in spoken languages, but in one hundred other languages, which include: imitation, the visual arts, sound, logical thought, metaphors, movement and many more. All these forms of expression and communication are valuable, for each one has its own eloquence and possibilities. A team of educators (*pedagogistas*) and artists (*atelieristas*) is affiliated with the schools and children's centres, now numbering 33. The Reggio Emilia approach has inspired many people throughout the world over time.

> The best thing we can do is learn from the children *themselves* how they learn.
> Loris Magaluzzi

The three educators
In the Reggio Emilia philosophy, children are each other's 'first educator': they learn most from each other. Adults are seen as the 'second educator' and the environment is seen as the 'third educator'. The environment is designed in such a way as to stimulate creativity. There is also always a studio available for the children.

Children are focused on communication; they research the world around them through their interactions with each other, and with the adults and their surroundings. In Reggio Emilia, they respond to this by arranging for children to work in small groups, which gives the very best chance of mutual exchange. That way, children learn from each other, about themselves and about the world.

IMG. 2.8 and 2.9 Examples of two older children in the Villa Comenius studio (inspired by Arno Stern) in Berlin, each painting in their own way, without a predetermined theme. One child has expanded the painting to include four pieces of paper, and wants to continue working on it next week. The other child paints the whole piece of paper and wonders aloud what colour lightning is; first painting with white, then yellow on top, all the while making lightning noises.

<<, <

The Reggio Emilia approach is based on a reflective cycle: research, watch and listen to what happens, record that, interpret the children's process, reflect and research further. It is a structural way of working with groups of children on a certain subject taken from the children's world. It can last for weeks or months. Adults are tasked with carefully and consciously setting up an inspiring environment in which children are researching.

The relationship between adults and children in Reggio Emilia is one of equivalence, and, at the same time, there are clear agreements and rules. There is room for progression precisely due to this combination.

In order to ascertain how children build their knowledge, everything in Reggio Emilia is about looking and listening carefully. The entire research process is recorded in words and images, including the adults' contributions. To achieve good planning, the educators discuss their personal observations and interpretations with each other.

Despite great enthusiasm for the Reggio Emilia philosophy from many followers around the world, this approach seems to conflict with general thinking on children's knowledge and learning. The basic preconditions are often lacking: facilitating children's research under an equivalent supervision is still far from commonplace, and mostly, there are no studios either.

If we look at traditional visual arts education, there is a persistent culture of handicrafts in which adults show children how to make something. Educators may think they are helping children by providing a picture to colour, or an example or a programme. Reggio Emilia takes as its starting point that which children *themselves* bring to the table, based on their own context. Subjects suggested by children are meaningful and understandable because they are their own

questions and ideas. This is why these subjects motivate far more than the themes suggested by adults. The visual language that children develop is richer and more authentic, precisely because they have not been offered pre-formed images. Because of this, their powers of expression and imagination will flourish.

2.2 The practice-oriented approach *Understanding Through Your Hands*

Juul, Stern and Reggio Emilia

Jesper Juul's vision, with its notion of equivalence and authenticity, is very much in line with the Reggio Emilia approach. Arno Stern's non-judgemental way of working, refraining from giving the child 'empty compliments', also ties in with the Reggio Emilia philosophy. His assertion that children carry their themes within was one of the major starting points for our vision.

As far as creative activities are concerned, an out-dated attitude towards the child might involve: 'What do you know about how to draw? How good are you at drawing? Hey, are you still scribbling? How far along are you in your development now, and is that good or not?' The new attitude should be to educate a child without judgement, but with a genuine interest in how they see the world. How does the child approach the material, how do they discover details, or possibilities that you might never have thought of? We would like to invite adults to be curious about the rich powers of children's imaginations, and enjoy the intensity of their research. Above all, we wish to learn from children. Children need us to be educators who take a position of equivalence, not one of assessor. They need us to give them options, and the time, peace and materials that will both challenge

and interest them. It takes quite a lot of mental effort to let go of the idea that children need themes, judgement and interpretation. Some adults may feel they are failing them, because they think that the child will learn nothing in those circumstances while others immediately assume it will lead to chaos. But it is only when we actually let go of old ideas on teaching, that children are able to express themselves, and flourish creatively. This is important for the development of their self-esteem.

Crescendo: from simple to more comprehensive

Workshops and training sessions about the approach of *Understanding Through Your Hands,* show that many adults want to explore and deepen their comprehension of the principles of creative work without predetermined themes, but they are not sure how and where to start. In order to keep things practical, feasible and organised, we advocate starting simply: by trying something on a small scale and gradually expanding it. That way, it stays accessible both for yourself and the children. With this in mind, we suggest the 'crescendo plan': start small and work towards big.

Crescendo = from small ⟨ to **large**

From showing restraint to researching together

If you want to achieve a high level of learning through discovery, start with the basis: equivalence. Children can learn a lot from adults, and adults can learn a lot from children. This means taking an attitude of holding back and refraining from lecturing: speech is generally silver; silence is sometimes golden. Well-intentioned remarks sometimes have the opposite effect. Be a 'witness' to what happens, register it. Assignments and judgements do not fit with the thinking behind equivalence. Intense focus, a safe and trusted atmosphere, pleasure and respect, do. Based on this idea, an 'I know best' relationship can slowly shift to an equivalent one. Enter into the dialogue with a child one step at a time, at the level of asking and researching together. Only introduce your knowledge when the child or the situation requires it.

> In order to place the initiative with the children, we have to unlearn various things: helping children when they are able to solve something themselves, or showing them how to do something. Judging something to be right or wrong, or saying you think something is beautiful does not belong here either.
> Huisingh et al. 2009

From a small group to autonomously making free work in a class

The younger the children, the smaller the group. That way, children grow accustomed to working confidently without a theme or assignment – it becomes a 'culture'. Children have to become familiar with this freedom. If they regularly work in this way, they become more independent and the group size can increase.

Materials: from few to many, from small to large

The crescendo plan also applies to the materials you work with. If an adult finds that guiding the creative processes is a challenge – 'I'm working like crazy' – there is something not right. Starting with fewer materials, fewer children and on a smaller scale, offers adults the chance to try things out. For children, fewer and smaller sizes are easier to handle and oversee, rather than an abundance of materials in all sizes and colours.

Drawing on a small size, such as A6, is a good start, inspiring and intensifying, for all ages. Later, they can work on a larger format but at the beginning, a large white sheet often arouses expectations. Repeatedly taking a small, new sheet is less results-orientated, particularly for very young children. A small piece of paper allows each child to work at their own pace. It invites experimentation, and is excellent for getting focused and into the flow. Small formats are also easier to dry and archive.

IMG. 2.10
<<<
Using simple materials such as sticks, string and inspiring photos from real life, children can shape their own ideas and knowledge about boats and shipping.

IMG. 2.11
<
This studio case from Atelier in een Koffer (Studio in a Case) contains everything you need to draw, paint and research materials. You can get to work with it straight away, either indoors or out. It contains mainly A6 pieces of paper so that children can work on a small scale. Later, they sometimes move on to working in a larger format, as shown on the easels in the background.

IMG. 2.12
Offering paper in a smaller format gives children the chance to get focused and into the flow. Not only that, it makes the large number of drawings that children produce manageable, for they can now be bound into mark-making books. Once children get going, they often spend a long time working and progress to exploring on a larger sheet of paper too.

IMG. 2.13 From small to big also means: going from elementary techniques, such as drawing and painting, to specific techniques such as working three-dimensionally with wood, stone or other materials. That way, you support children to become familiar with the abundance of possibilities to be found in expressing themselves on a sheet of white paper, plus you make it more manageable for yourself. You can draw pretty much anywhere but working with voluminous materials or complicated techniques requires more preparation, knowledge, time and storage.

Less is more

Drawing is a key activity. Research shows that children who draw and paint reinforce the centres of the brain, activate their neural networks and develop ways of observing and thinking that help them mature later on.
Mieras 2009

Little or few does not necessarily mean less valuable. Little is the start of something that can grow. One sheet of paper and one pencil can be the start of a myriad of other resources with which children can shape their imagination. And if it stays little: that's fine too, just as long as it intrigues.

Offering all the material you have at your disposal all at once is too much. Children will be unable to choose; they won't know where to begin. It makes good sense to start off with one or two things and gradually expand the choice of materials. This way the children's process is deepened and they can get into a flow.

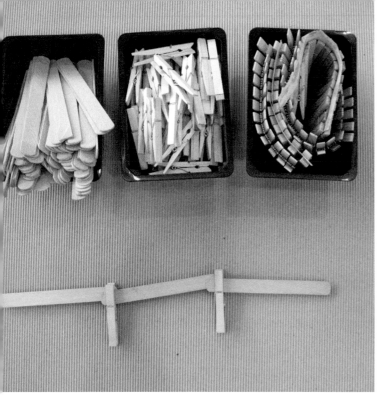

IMG. 2.14   It often suffices to offer two or three materials; water and cardboard, for example, or sticks and clothes pegs with wood glue. Limiting materials gives a definite framework. Not too much to choose from, which may cause stress or mess, but something achievable and inspiring, due to the simplicity.

Lastly

From the moment a child is born into this world, they will assess whether something is pleasant or unpleasant, before considering whether they find something right or wrong. Fundamental experiences of whether something is pleasant or unpleasant form the basis of the child's entire development. Later, much of what children observe is provided in their upbringing or at school. Young children are scarcely permitted to observe – that which they experience is soon given a cognitive or moral judgement.
Liebau 2010

Anyone searching on the Internet using the terms 'arts and crafts for children', will find thousands of examples of extremely colourful art and craft ideas. Usually, without exception, they are all crafted objects that have been thought up and made almost entirely by adults. They often include accompanying templates and step-by-step instructions, or demonstration videos for achieving a pre-planned result.

If educators do not critically evaluate the educative value of an experience, activities may be justified only for their fun, mess or entertainment value. Materials will be limited in their quality and in their capacity to make meaningful, rich marks

IMG. 2.15   After drawing on A6 cards for half an hour, these children work autonomously on a large format at the easel. Crescendo: from small to large.

and may also be excessively commercial or designed for one specific use. The scope for individual learning, growth and creative expression is diminished. The educator may be extremely hands-on in such activities; however, their hands-on role will be to manage or even to make the item for children, particularly if the product has been selected as a class-wide thematic or seasonal product. Such activities seek to keep children busy and entertained, to meet perceived parents' expectations or to satisfy the educator's desire to make a product for special events and celebrations.
Lindsay 2016

Many parents and educators all over the world set great store by cognitive achievement at an increasingly young age. In some cases, testing is encouraged from the age of three in childcare centres. And, when a child fails to meet an average quickly enough, more often than not there's panic: help, a learning deficit!

Various scientific research (Goorhuis-Brouwer 2010, 2012; Jolles 2011) suggests that children do not become more malleable by being tested and assessed. What is needed is for their social-emotional well-being to be nurtured, fostering a sound sense of self-esteem. This is a fundamental requirement for healthy development.

You also learn from visual arts, music, dance and drama. As experiences, they are on a par with arithmetic, language, history and world orientation. Visual subjects in particular are suitable for learning presentation skills, practising how to receive applause, collaboration and developing pleasure in learning. They benefit self-esteem. This kind of learning is not about 'scoring' achievements, but about acquiring knowledge through your senses and further developing that knowledge. The role of the adult is consequently not to deploy methods, but rather to observe children and associate with them.
Baeyens 2011

It would be wonderful if both governments and education were to give sustainable arts education the status it deserves, and acknowledge that it can greatly contribute to the development of self-esteem and personality in every child. In the future, we will need people who are flexible and able to solve complex problems. This develops through creative learning and by focusing in particular on the foundations: non-lecturing and equivalence. Above all, the emphasis is on providing choice and space for learning through discovery. Only then can learning be mutually enjoyable and effective.

This book hopes to be a step in that direction. Not by wanting to achieve the unattainable, but by realising the goal step by step. For example, you might begin by scheduling a theme-free, creative experience once a week. A team could also agree to organise week-long projects each year, which focus on materials research and learning through discovery. A subsequent (or initial) step could be to set up a permanent studio space (preferably with a subject teacher) and to give it a prominent place in the curriculum.

IMG. 2.16   After drawing on A6 cards for about half an hour, 4–6-year-old children are very enthusiastic to draw
>   on an old big lampshade, talking about what and how they draw; learning from one another. The
           drawing at the bottom right depicts the war in Ukraine, showing that serious topics can arise, which
           you may not expect.

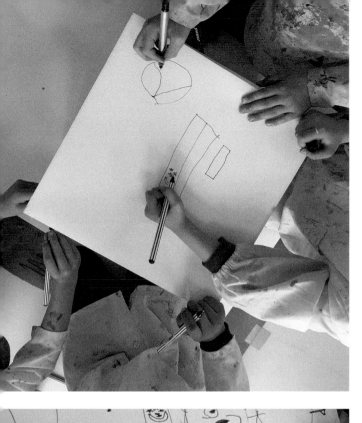

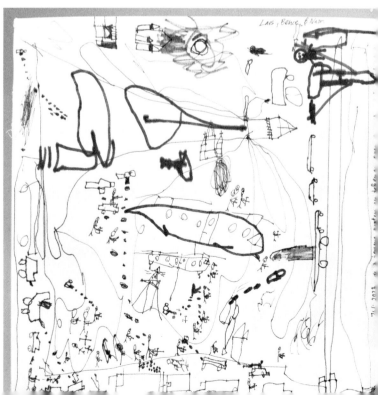

3 Guiding creative processes

3.1 Introduction

You might have the most fantastic creative spaces, but in the end, it's not only about what there is to see and experience, it is also about the way adults and children interact. Adults determine what opportunities children are given. Adults are responsible for the atmosphere, the time, the tranquillity, the space, the preparations and the materials. *They* determine the way children are allowed to work.

Adults who want to teach children have a task that is both modest *and* deciding. *Modest* because with adults, speech is generally silver and silence is golden. By this, we mean it is crucial not to immediately begin by giving assignments or instructions, but to first give children the opportunity to make marks and observe how they approach the material. Adults are also *deciding*. For example, they establish the extent to which children can experiment and research. They do this by offering time, space and materials etc., so that children can give full rein to their urges to explore and experiment. It is also crucial that adults avoid disturbing or distracting children while they are immersed in play (e.g. 'Clear everything away!' or 'Would you like something to drink?' or 'Why is that traffic light blue?').

Children who are given room to think for themselves, and, for example, go about making something, are being challenged to use their brains in a different way. This is more likely to happen when there is less of a directed strategy or plan. At school, children tend to learn to think in a more instructional and targeted way. Associative and intuitive ideas that bubble up during experimentation cannot be approached and steered in such a direct way. This means, therefore, that you need to let go of the idea of reaching a goal in fixed stages, and trust that things will progress and be fine in the end.

3.2 Basic attitudes, responsibilities and tasks of adults

Can anyone do this?

Whether you are a parent, teacher, educator or student, everyone who recognises the importance of mark-making has the potential to support and work creatively with children. This begins with the basics: being non-judgemental; beginning simply with a few materials; working in small groups; and keeping a selection of materials or tools to one side, in order to extend and deepen the process as you go along. After that, it is an ongoing learning experience for both the children and the adults, and each adult can develop their own way of working with *How Children Learn and Create Using Art, Play and Science: Understanding Through Your Hands*. Sometimes, adults shy away from creative activities, perhaps because they are worried it may involve a

IMG. 3.1   Studio educator Nicole Roel in the Princes Juliana Children's Centre studio in Amsterdam.
<

IMG. 3.3   Left: little dishes containing macaroni, papier mâché, wooden dolls, caps, bits of fabric, wooden sticks and paste. Right: the results of a whole morning of researching and experimenting.

lot of work or mess. Perhaps there is anxiety about complicated techniques or which handicraft to choose? The great thing about working in a theme-free way, is that there is no need to think up or fill-in anything for the children. Instead, as a start, focus on some basic but good quality drawing materials and office tools such as a neon marker, a stapler or a hole punch. If you offer these regularly, it won't be boring, but you might be surprised what children will come up with.

It can sometimes be thought that it is not worthwhile providing drawing materials, particularly if you think children only want to draw for five or ten minutes. But this is not the case, for it is only when children have regular opportunities to draw, that they really get to know the materials and accompanying possibilities.

3.2.1   Creating an inspiring atmosphere

Inspired
Children get inspired by the atmosphere, their surroundings and materials. This is usually an unconscious process. When directly invited: 'Would you like to draw?', a child might well say 'No'. Then again, by saying nothing and putting a piece of paper and a felt-tipped pen on the table, this may happen of its own accord.

I actually always have something that triggers or tempts them, something they find really exciting. Today I have test tubes and things to smell and taste. All kinds of herbs, lemon, yoghurt, water, vanilla and things

IMG. 3.2   You can inspire and amaze children at home: lay a sheet of paper and some felt-tipped pens on
<   an empty desk. Children don't always plan to draw but if the situation invites them to, they will
spontaneously pick up a pen and begin…

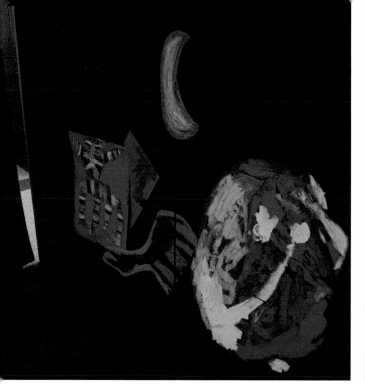

IMG. 3.5   An exciting atmosphere can be created with light and dark. Left: fluorescent paint in a dark room. Right: a light box with sand to write or draw in.

like that. And all sorts of jars, funnels and tweezers too. I just lay it all out and watch what happens. That works with most children but not always, and not with everyone. If I had an idea beforehand of how it would work, that's when it mostly goes wrong. But if I let go of that, if I can see that what I didn't expect is also great, things go well again.
Sanne Groen, Westerdok Children's Centre, Amsterdam

About the choice of materials – children will soon become intrigued by *simple* materials and natural or technical objects and phenomena. They will be curious, and want to study everything: for example, sounds, light, colours, reflections and movement. This may include materials, such as a box, a stick, a container full of sand, water, paint, a piece of fabric, or perhaps, something that shines or sparkles. Wonder and excitement play a part, for example with a bucket of water, some small bowls and a kitchen strainer or funnel.

Beauty

Creating atmosphere and beauty go hand in hand. Beauty comes from thinking, imagining and being aware of your own 'sense of beauty'. Beauty is something you feel from within, not from an objective assessor. This is where the difference lies – between something that someone else finds 'beautiful', and personally being contented with what

IMG. 3.4   What one person finds beautiful, another may find kitsch. What one person finds exciting, another may
<   find boring. Everyone has a sense of beauty or ugliness, including children. This cupboard full of metal objects and technical equipment might not appeal to every child, but some will love it.

IMG. 3.6   Playing in an enticing play environment: the prepared environment immediately invites children to get started at the drawing table.

you have made. It is important for children to develop their own sense of beauty, without being dependent on the judgement of others. Beauty does not just involve art, clothing or jewellery; it can be found everywhere. For example, mathematicians speak of 'an elegant formula'.

Beauty means sensitivity to the relationships between people and things. Sensitivity to the daily process that helps us feel 'how things dance together'.
Vecchi 2010

The first experiences of beauty are in your youth. Children live, as do adults, not in a world as it really is, but in a world as they personally perceive it.
Liebau 2010

Prepared environment

For the adults whose job it is to create a positive atmosphere where children will immediately want to get involved, the following questions are worth considering: How do you design the space? What sort of layout will work best? Which materials will you choose to offer? To create an enticing environment, materials must be presented in such a way that they appeal to children's curiosity, their sense of wonder and their imagination. It will also help to offer smaller selections of materials, so these remain manageable for the children and they do not become over-stimulated. A neutral surface to work on will enable the focus to stay on the materials and discovery. Attractive spaces will be created by the thoughtful presentation of materials; the natural beauty of these will stimulate and fire the imagination (see also IMG. 3.43 with 9 examples of a prepared environment).

IMG. 3.7 A prepared environment at a school with 4 workstations to choose from: at the back right of the photo, the drawing table with each child's research book lying ready (see IMG. 3.6). At the back left, there is a table with a large sheet of paper stuck down, and wax crayons; later, there will be liquid water colours or saltshakers, for example, for working in more depth. At the front left, there is salt bread dough (three green balls); later in the process, tools can be added for the next level. At the front right, there is a selection of building materials with different kinds of sticky tape and open-ended recycling materials (make sure everything is free of advertising, to keep distracting triggers to a minimum). You could cover this station with a large cloth in the beginning, so that the focus is initially on the drawing table and play stations, and to help encourage concentration.

Presenting triggers

Avoid presenting materials altogether in a big chest. Preferably, arrange them on the floor or tabletop in smaller dishes or baskets. Or you might organise them on a large tray or a mirror, stacked up or in a circle. Materials that you keep initially hidden under a cloth or in a box will also help to focus attention.

Selection to choose from

Offering at least two workstations will give children the chance to make their own choices. You might start all together at the drawing table, and after a while let those who are finished move to another, prepared workstation, so that they can carry on independently. For example, this could be painting on a large-scale at easels, or an area set up to freely explore buttons or a constructing area with cardboard and glue.

You can also start with a natural clay or salt bread dough. All these stations are ready and inviting. This clear framework makes it possible for children to choose – they do not have to all make the same thing

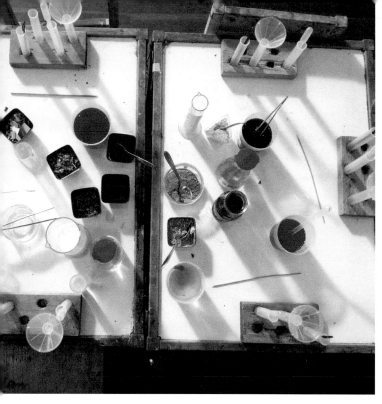

Salt breaddough:
2 × flour
1 × salt
1 × water
(poss. oil)

Rijgen, met natuurlijke en recycle materialen

IMG. 3.9   The prepared studio at Kris Kras Atelier de Pijp in Amsterdam.

and they have space to move around. Often, children will re-visit the drawing table or one of the other workstations after a while.

> Adults don't always come up with the idea of using materials in different ways. Why not try it? For instance, you might use the reverse, or turn things inside out or upside down or back to front! Consider unusual combinations; thread everything that has a hole in it, or paint with water. 'I work with anything and everything: recently with the combination of clay and scissors. You see the children thinking: 'Can you cut that?'. I had put out a big block of clay, rather than small, ready-to-use pieces. They had to pull it apart themselves and they cut bits off with the scissors. You have to supervise well; watch carefully what they're doing, how they're doing it, and ask if they need anything.
> Tihana Trputec, Altijd Lente Children's Centre, Amsterdam

IMG. 3.8   When we say a prepared environment, it could be assumed that this is a perfectly arranged space.
<   However, it is best if it is not too full or colourful, and that it appears restful. That way, children will be able to concentrate on the material. Examples of a prepared environment clockwise from top left to right: experimenting with liquids and powders, making salt bread dough with the children (2 parts flour + 1 part salt + 1 part water), threading with beads and recycled materials, natural clay with kitchen utensils.

Pattern for a painting smock
1 sheet = 2 painting smocks

Fold fabric double here

37.40 inch

3.94 inch

3.94 inch

6 inch

Cut 6 inch
at the back

23.62 inch

21.65 inch

Cut the smock out following the blue lines and
sew up the side seams.

Inspiring spaces

It is wonderful to have a special place where children are allowed to work creatively. The valuable thing is that they are able to *concentrate* there. In one large open space where, in addition to creative activities, all sorts of other things are going on, the children can often become distracted. It will be ideal to make use of a separate basement area, or an upper floor or attic, or a small room.

Kitchen or outdoor 'studios'

Parents and host parents may, in particular, have some good options. Working creatively in small groups may be easier, as they will probably be with just one, two or three children. Perhaps a kitchen area will provide a relaxed space where children can make a bit of a mess and where there are all kinds of materials and tools to hand. The 'ideal' workplace for these sorts of activities does

IMG. 3.10   Here are a few 'make it yourself' tips. From top left to right: you can make your own easel using a
<   trestle, a large board and two straight screw hooks (see inset for image of screw). Children often respond spontaneously to office material, such as a hole puncher, sticky tape or markers. From bottom left to right: instead of buying plastic painting smocks, you can easily make comfortable cotton ones yourself (see diagram). And with just two sheets of paper on a fence, an inviting garden studio is ready to use.

IMG. 3.11   Do-it-yourself tip for the studio: recycled disposable sauce cups in a former beer tray. It stops the cups from tipping over. For applying paint: paint-rollers, feathers, toothbrushes and small and large paint brushes.

not exist. There will always be limitations, so it is a case of making best use of what you have. Working outside, either in a garden or on the beach may not seem like an obvious choice, but it can be surprisingly successful. Making a mess outside is generally not a problem.

A studio for children

The word 'studio' is often used in the Reggio Emilia approach for the special place where children can develop their creative ideas in small groups. It is usually a central place in every children's centre or pre-school. The word 'studio' can be a little off-putting, because, just as the word 'art', it can sound strange. But it defines a space where children are allowed to research, draw and experiment freely, facilitated by an artist. By being allowed to express themselves there, together with other children, they sharpen their observation skills, and learn from each other and from the materials. Materials will usually be natural or recycled resources, and are often known as open-ended materials. You see the marks of learning processes in the studios. For adults, that is precisely *the* key to seeing which route children take to forming their ideas and accumulating knowledge about the world.

3.2.2   Choice of material

The strength lies in the simplicity

Children are intrigued by materials that they can explore by using all of their senses. It's not yet about a result, it's about feeling and touching, smelling, tasting, looking and listening. It is essential that the materials evoke amazement and curiosity: 'Hey, what's this?'. The motto is: the simpler, the better. Just one large cardboard box can be the basis of a whole morning of research.

> I have sometimes worked for more than an hour with the children with a box full of bottle tops. They think it's fantastic when I put them into containers. They put the tops into things, sort them into colours… They're 'magic powers' to them, that's what they call it. And I join in with that: 'I've seen your magic powers; shall we look for them?' Then all you have to do is watch what happens. Often, interactions will be generated. They lay the tops in a long line and they sort them into colours, put them into things and count them. The boys in particular really like material like this.
> Claudia Zinnemers, Uit de kunst Daycare Centre, Amersfoort

A lot of one kind

It is surprising, and also enticing for children of all ages, to offer a large amount of one type of material, rather than smaller amounts of many different types. With stones, for example, there are many options: bits of rock, marble or other kinds of stone, polished stones, large pebbles or coarse sand. This offers children the opportunity to count,

IMG. 3.12   Cardboard is a simple but extremely versatile material for all age groups.
<

IMG. 3.13   Selection of hard, soft and flexible materials.
>

IMG. 3.14   Many adults can remember playing with their mother's button jar.
>>

IMG. 3.15   Examples of open-ended materials. Basic shapes can always be found in these – see if you can
>>>   recognise lines, dots, circles, sun shapes and arches.

IMG. 3.16   String, thread and ribbon can be used in multiple ways. Knitting and sewing are obvious choices, but there are other possibilities, for example: drawing, connecting things together, decorating, plaiting and binding.

sort, categorise, combine and mix, as well as create shapes and patterns. Buttons are fantastic for all sorts of activities: children use them for a whole myriad of mathematical activities, including games and story-making.

Open-ended material

Open-ended materials are materials that can be used for more than one purpose. For example, a bobbin can be a chimney, a doll, a vase, a stamp or a tree trunk to name but a few! Open-ended materials speak to a child's power of imagination as opposed to materials with just one purpose: a fire engine is a fire engine and nothing else.

The same goes for images: if children are offered pictures of a fish to colour in, or stickers with aeroplanes or butterflies, you have taken away their chance to come up with their own ideas or representations of these. Children are masters of associating, imagining and abstract thinking: for instance, a plank can become a bridge; a box a house, or a pile of flour can become a snowy landscape.

Basic shapes

When you look closely, open-ended materials can be seen to contain the basic shapes of visual language: a line, a dot, a circle, an arch or a spiral. These are the

IMG. 3.17   From top left to right: these children are working intensively with a shoelace and cooked spaghetti, in
>   which the basic 'line' shape can be seen. From bottom left to right: when building with boxes, the basic shape of a rectangle is noticeable. A boy is connecting two strips of cardboard with sticky tape to form a cross – this is another basic shape.

IMG. 3.18 Look at the photos of all the different materials in this chapter and notice the basic shapes hidden in them.

IMG. 3.19 To let the children connect things together, I often use double-sided sticky tape, the kind you can easily tear with your fingers. You use it for sticking down carpet too. It's particularly effective for three-dimensional work with plastic materials, less expensive than glue and works really well (Monique Eilertsen, Scrap XL recycle shop, Rotterdam).

IMG. 3.20   When out walking, it can be helpful to have some small bags with you for collecting materials.

foundational shapes that children use to construct a drawing. For example, a child will draw a person based on circles, dots and lines. Open-ended materials are therefore ideal, and will give children many opportunities to make links and associations. E.g., they may create a person from a lid (circle), sticks (lines) and stones (dots). As well as appealing to the imagination, these sorts of materials are both inexpensive and sustainable.

Connecting material

The value of connecting materials during creative activities can sometimes be underestimated. When one material is connected to another, something new is created. So connecting material should always be in stock and to hand. This can include long strips, such as coloured sticky tape with which you can 'draw', or wool, thread, elastic, cord, wide tape, ribbon and string. Children can become fascinated by sticky tape,

for example, and there are various types to try: paper or plastic, coloured, transparent or double-sided. Children can tear paper tape themselves or use scissors to cut with. Other connecting materials will include clothes pegs, glue and wallpaper paste. Children are often fascinated by 'drawing' with glue in a bottle. Putting wallpaper paste in empty honey or ketchup squeezy bottles (see IMG. 3.27) will allow them to 'draw' as much as they like without it getting too expensive.

Natural materials

It is worthwhile collecting natural materials both due to their calming, simple effect, and their interesting appearance. Things such as sticks, stones and various types of sand therefore make up a basic set in the studio. Other natural materials such as cocoa shells, bird sand, hay or seeds can be found in garden centres or pet shops.

Seek and ye shall find

Children frequently enjoy collecting objects and other items, and these can be found filling their pockets. The street, park or woods can be great places to gather all kinds of treasure – look out for different sorts of sand, leaves, feathers, stones, snail shells, pieces of bark, twigs, beech nuts, chestnuts or shells to add to your collections. Local companies can also be a good source of free and found, for example, bicycle tyres cut into pieces are an unusual and fascinating material.

> We recently painted twigs – the children are so proud of them. They hang them up themselves and other bits and bobs can be added to them. I had picked up a child from school who had been wanting to look for twigs for a long time and now was the right moment. You come back with armfuls of twigs and branches. Children from another school said: 'Wow, there's a whole pile of twigs and branches here' and got straight to work. That's just really spontaneous. You don't think it up in advance. I did have a sneaking suspicion that we could do something with twigs but no more than that.
> Tanja Sap, Kikonia, Outside School Care, Rotterdam

Simple, interesting and exciting material that costs little or nothing

- foodstuffs such as rice, pasta, couscous, lentils (past sell-by date or left-overs)
- lids, caps and bottle tops, in all shapes and sizes
- cans (opened with a can opener and with no sharp rim)
- clean packaging materials without advertising, containers and dishes (preferably stackable)
- preserving jars or large glass jars for storing materials attractively

IMG. 3.21   Balls of wool are surprising toys for young children.

- old bicycle tyres, wheels, nuts and bolts, buttons, metal rings, old postage stamps (technical and genuine materials from daily life)
- dried flowers, seeds, pips, pinecones or other nature finds or left-over kitchen supplies
- stiff paper (at least 180 gr./6.3 ounce) left-overs from printing companies, preferably A6 format
- cardboard cut into small pieces and various sizes of cardboard cylinders
- sticks and stones in all colours and sizes and various kinds of sand, fun to collect with the children.

Safe and challenging material for babies

For babies, household products such as flour, corn or potato starch, water, herbs, food colouring (diluted in glue or water), tea, potatoes, seeds, coconut milk, whipped cream, yoghurt, cooked spaghetti and all

IMG. 3.22 Open-ended materials such as stiff white papers and natural clay leave a lot of scope for children's imagination. Brightly coloured paper or plasticine can be distracting and fail to take children's creative ability seriously.

kinds of rice, pulses and pasta are intriguing and safe materials. They allow children to discover using all their senses. It's not a waste when using very small amounts and reusing the dry foodstuffs again and again. Here too, you will find basic shapes within the materials.

Tools and material: real is better than fake

Provide real, good quality tools for children to work with. These will appeal to children who will recognise them from the adult world. Painting materials from a professional art suppliers will usually be superior to children's tools. These are worth investing in and will last longer. Intriguing materials can be presented in glass, metal, wood or wicker containers instead of the more familiar, coloured plastic ones. Real clay with wooden hammers and sieves will be far more interesting than plasticine with plastic moulds. From around the age of eighteen months, children can already handle appropriately sized scissors, paint rollers, scouring pads, shaving brushes, toothbrushes, combs or brushes made from a stick and foam rubber. This will support them to become familiar with tools and learn to

IMG. 3.23 Top photos: Children are taken seriously when they are given tools and materials that are also used by
> professionals, such as a vice, a saw and a hammer and nails.

IMG. 3.24 Bottom photos: Materials, such as wire, plaster, aluminium and natural clay are sourced from DIY stores
> and art supply shops. In the same way, tools, such as sieves, scoops and funnels, are multifunctional
  and far more interesting than brightly coloured plastic sand moulds.

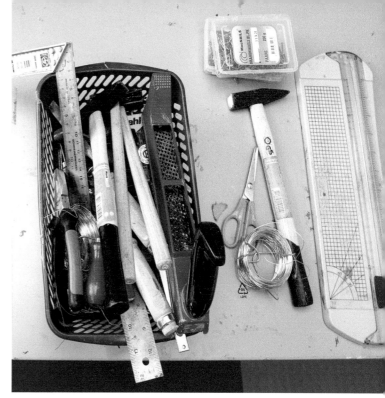

use them well. Toddlers will enjoy working with pipettes, plastic test tubes and shakers.

Storage: cupboards, containers

Well-stored materials will not only provide an overview of what is available, but also offer tranquillity, which both children and adults will find inviting. For instance, a tall, well-organised cupboard with labelled crates will help adults to see at a glance where things are. This will make it easier to find equipment and tidy-up, and also make for a pleasing environment.

IMG. 3.25 << A deep cupboard, open or closed, is indispensable. Labels or pictures of what is contained within will make materials easy to find. Bottom left: Drying racks are really handy for drying out large sheets of paper. Bottom right: A floor to ceiling rack, with more than 100 uniform containers, in the Atelier in een Koffer studio in Amsterdam.

IMG. 3.26 < Avoid the creative cliché of chaos in your cupboard. Cut up materials in small pieces for overview and compact storage.

IMG. 3.27 Plastic plant containers are space-saving and useful: placed in a deep cupboard with the short side to the front, they can hold a lot. Right: wallpaper paste mixed with paint in squeezy bottles is a fun and sustainable way of exploring glue and sticking.

First make small

Larger items can be cut down into smaller, more manageable pieces that will be easier to store. With the children's help, a wicker lampshade can be sawn into bits, or the pine-cones collected from the Christmas tree. By making objects smaller, it again allows a focus on basic shapes: pine cones have lines, tube slices are circular, and wooden blocks are rectangular. Materials in smaller pieces speak directly to the imagination.

Presenting just a small amount of materials in containers or glasses avoids the need for large quantities, and having to use valuable space for storage. Clearing up is easier, and children will enjoy the exciting possibilities the materials have to offer. A small container is more accessible and can quickly be re-filled. Applying the 'less is more' principle, we have found that with fewer things lying around children focus better, their fine motor skills are automatically called-upon, and the energy is calm.

Don't go mad…

It is easy to get carried away with enthusiasm for so many interesting resources and their potential. Consider practicalities and be flexible. Collecting, sorting and storing a variety of different size materials takes time, space and energy. Though desirable to have a studio and a large storage cupboard, these are not absolutely necessary. If not available, concentrate on mark-making with drawing and painting, and use household and natural materials. Shoeboxes make perfect containers – they are easy to stock and store, and make working with open-ended materials manageable. Inspiring materials should be a help, not a hindrance.

Tidying regularly will be part of creating an attractive ambience. Though perhaps a less enjoyable part of the job, it can also be very satisfying to create a space that radiates tranquillity and order. A child's desk at home, cleared, or a tidy studio in a children's centre or school also results in a cleared mind. That goes for both adults and children. A selection of similar robust storage boxes will be a great investment.

3.2.3   Individual guidance and getting children into the flow

Small groups

Working in small groups is an important prerequisite if you wish to give personal attention and build concentration. A group of 4 children is ideal. As numbers increase, it becomes more difficult to support the children's attention or give individual guidance. When older children have regular opportunities to work independently, they will be able to do this for longer periods and within larger groups.

Talk (don't)

In order to encourage children to get into the flow, it will help to keep talk to a minimum. Take a position of restraint – even if you are enthusiastic, be careful not to overwhelm children. Allow the children to 'wait and see', and try things out. Shy children will need time to watch without the pressure of having to join in. If they are given opportunities to initiate things for themselves, this will build trust in the adults, in the space and in the exploration of the materials. This is likely to result in them expressing themselves more frequently with greater confidence.

IMG. 3.28   In order to introduce children to challenging materials regularly, and to keep things viable for the
<   educator, materials are best presented in small containers and jars. That way, clearing up is limited to washing up a dish of small items.

IMG. 3.31   Some children start scribbling and drawing straight away, others play 'wait and see'. This is to be expected – children will be put at ease and develop their confidence by not being pushed too quickly, too soon.

Each at their own pace
Each child has their own pace. Some may find it difficult to concentrate for periods of longer than ten minutes, whilst others – of the same age – might work on for an hour or more. If intrigued, children will stay deeply involved. Don't rush them – if a child finishes early, your challenge is to tempt them with other material or tools to keep working or start something new. Once you've got them interested, they will get into (the) flow and do not want to stop anymore.

Having them concentrate
You have created a good ambience, and have every faith in the children; you have considered your materials, presenting them carefully and aesthetically. The children seem interested – is this all there is to it? Is it possible to sit back and watch what happens now, or, is there still an essential task so children stay focused on their work?

Unaccustomed at the beginning
Note well! It is precisely these first fifteen minutes that are crucial in starting up a creative process. Some children might get going straight away, and involve others. Less confident children require a gentler approach, with time and space for them to begin. Few words and less direct attention is often the best way.

IMG. 3.29   Helping both a shy and a boisterous child to become focused is a special challenge for the studio
<<   educator.

IMG. 3.30   For a young child, drawing means trying things out and making their own marks. Looking, feeling
<   and making a mess are all part of this, even the elementary task of taking the lid on and off a
              felt-tipped pen ten times.

IMG. 3.32   Drawing with a black marker. It is essential to have a number of roller pens and thick markers in stock as basic materials. The contrast between white paper and a single black pen invites a child to draw clear lines. With less distraction from colours, they can concentrate fully on the line.

Just the right balance of attention and encouragement will make the difference between a child feeling comfortable or ill at ease. You may notice that in the first fifteen minutes, children feel a little awkward, and take their time to start. Don't be discouraged, this is normal. Children (and adults, too) need time to get used to a new situation. Being able to watch others is a valuable step – so too, is the rule that even if you are not yet working, it is not okay to disturb those who are.

Drawing and painting are not boring

Drawing and painting on a small scale (A6 cards) are good ways to develop concentration. If you want children to get in flow, always start with that. Then you can progress to something else. Scribbling and drawing are fundamental ways of making marks – every child can participate of their own accord, without instruction.

> Drawing means taking a line for a walk.
> Paul Klee

I have a drawing book for each child in the classroom and they can draw whatever they like in it. Children receive absolutely no comments about those drawings. After some time, we look back on what is occupying the children, what marks they have made.
Hanneke Saaltink, Nicholaas Beetsschool, Alkmaar

With just a line and a dot, children can express meaning: a horizontal line becomes a bridge, a perpendicular line a person and a circle becomes a swimming pool. This is a symbolic-graphic language. This abstract visual language is often difficult for adults to 'read', just as written letters are an incomprehensible secret language for young children. However, it is important to take children's scribble and abstract drawings seriously. Children will understand their visual language, and that of other children. If they discover the basic shapes – circles, rectangles and spirals – through this process, they will continue to play and represent them. That way, they begin to identify different shapes with things in real life. These moments of recognition are full of pride – learning through discovery that results in 'wow' moments. If children are taught how they should draw a tree, or that grass is always green, they will not discover their own visual language. It will be a deterrent rather than an incentive; as if you are teaching a bizarre language.

Maintaining concentration

To support children's concentration, notice what it is they are doing. *Stay alert* and involved and let them continue working in the flow. You may need to offer them new sheets of paper, or other materials, and retreat but remain tuned in as they continue. Allow time for them to become familiar with the materials. When children find things that interest them, they can remain engaged for a long time. For example, this might be cutting with scissors, drawing with a special marker pen or taking the lid on and off a felt-tipped pen. When a child is engrossed in their explorations, there are often special moments of discovery. Enjoy – don't stand up or walk away. This is a moment to discreetly take photos or make notes.

> 10,000 scribbles are 10,000 neural connections.
> Titia Sprey

From mark-making on A6 paper to other workshop materials

It is very satisfying to see children maintaining focus for longer periods, for example if they are working from small to large. Often, children who first draw on A6 size paper become so engrossed that, after half an hour, they may wish to move on to painting on a larger scale. Then, it is as if they are just getting started! Or you can offer something else; salt dough, for example, or papier mâché. Once accustomed, children may be open to other, new experiences. Some might head back to the drawing table and reconnect with drawing. That's a compliment for you: it shows that your offer is working well – children are following their intuition, and refreshed by both the variety and the opportunity to return to something.

IMG. 3.33 This boy has begun painting. By gently offering new material at a certain moment, he discovers a
< watercolour pencil with water, then mixes flour in wet paint puddles and pours water on his sheet. These are usually chance marks that are made during this kind of research. He was occupied for a solid hour and worked on around ten A6 cards.

IMG. 3.34 When supporting, the educator must be alert to what each child might need and discreetly facilitate,
> often best without saying anything. Then children are not disturbed in their research.

In our children's studio in Berlin, we believe it's very important to take a break in order to be able to maintain concentration. When the group slowly became restless during painting, it was about time for that break. Anyone who wanted to continue working was allowed to and anyone who wanted, could go and play outside. In the afternoon, the group got together again and every child could talk about their painting. If anyone wanted to keep working on, in the afternoon, that was fine too. It sometimes happens that in this way, children work for three weeks on one painting.
Tanja Belder, Klax-Kindergarten, Berlijn

When supporting children, this is about much more than giving instructions. It is an active process, whereby you share their curiosity and enthusiasm for researching together. Only help when absolutely necessary. And introducing new things in response to what the children show you. It's not enough to just let them get on with it, or wait and see.
Jenthe Baeyens, De Wegwijzer Primary School, Groningen

3.2.4 Appreciating instead of judging, focusing on the process rather than the product

You offer them something they can focus on. You keep an eye on what appeals to them. Once they're in the flow, I don't interrupt them because you lose concentration if you're constantly being corrected or told how it should be done…
Jesse van de Hoogen, Uit de Kunst Childcare Centre, Amersfoort

Beware of saying 'beautiful' a hundred times

Supervising children in a non-judgemental way means not fussing about what they have made, but creating the optimum conditions for children to work and remain involved. It's important not to speak of lovely, nice, beautiful or wonderful or any other aesthetic judgement, however difficult that is in practice. Children who hear that something is beautiful will want to hear this again and again, and they will become dependent on your opinion. The priority is for children to follow their interests, to research and discover. As you listen to them, the connections they make will give you a glimpse into their personal world. This can be a sensitive moment that makes them vulnerable, and therefore, the right/wrong/beautiful label is simply not appropriate here.

Don't disturb concentration

Giving children space to concentrate on their creative activities means not disturbing them. The saying 'speech is silver but silence is golden' often applies. This gives room for interaction between the children, too. Children will learn through watching each other and talking together.

I feel the need to ask all sorts of questions, like: 'What are you making?'. But it's precisely by my saying nothing that the children can get on with their own activities and discover things themselves. While I am concentrating on making notes or sharpening pencils, they're concentrating and discovering.
Marit Rienstra, Mauritskade Childcare Centre, Amsterdam

Pitfalls to avoid when supervising children (based on De Valck 2012)

- Questions: *What are you making?* If a child makes connections whilst involved in making, they will let you know in their own time. They won't be able to answer questions whilst in the middle of a creative process. Rather than asking questions, make a note of any information the child volunteers.
- *Not listening* to what a child tells you, of their own accord, about the material or how they are experiencing it.
- *Comparing* one child's work with that of others. Everyone works in their own way, at their own pace and with their own visual language.
- Directing, by saying *how it should be or what the intention is.*
- *Interfering with a child's work*: drawing, painting, colouring or sticking clay somewhere, while they are still at work, or giving pointers: that goes there. Or worse: taking over actions. Children are in charge of their own work!
- Allowing *other adults* to wander into the creative space with all sorts of questions or comments about lovely or ugly. This will disturb children's concentration and process.

How and when you might ask questions

It is useful to know which questions to ask and when. Caution is required here, for to ask too many questions may signal to the child you want them to go in certain direction, or that you do not understand their work. A valid question is: 'Would you like to tell me something about it?' This gives a child the chance to say 'No'. Good questions will help to sharpen the senses, and prompt stimulation and challenge (De Valck 2012).

- Offer help: 'Do you need anything else?'
- Encourage them to focus: 'Do you hear/see/feel/taste/smell that too…?'
- Suggest a challenge: 'How would it be if you…?'
- Invite them to expand on what you see: 'Does it all turn the same way? What do you see?'
- Foster logical thinking: 'What could you use to do that? What would happen if…?'
- Challenge them to solve a problem: 'What could you use to make that?'

What can you do?

If explaining or directing, judging or asking closed questions is not on, adults often wonder what they *can* do. For example, you might:

- Pay attention to a child's involvement. Be curious about what they are doing or thinking.
- Affirm what they are doing: 'Gosh, you're hard at work!'
- Look at their technique: 'You have to be strong to cut, don't you?'
- Draw attention to the materials: 'How does that feel? Is it soft or rough?'
- Stay close to a child if they are having difficulty – do not underestimate the support your presence can provide. A child will feel seen and acknowledged, and perhaps dare to continue.

IMG. 3.35   When the adult avoids interrupting, children can learn a lot from one another. They are each other's first educator.

<

IMG. 3.36   Left: Andrea Flach of Villa Comenius (out-of-school care) in the painting studio in Berlin, supports the children and has faith in their capabilities. She encourages them by inviting them to answer their own questions, rather than offering solutions. Right: a girl approaches art teacher Tanja Belder in the Klax studio, Berlin and says: 'I've drawn it wrong'. Tanja replies: 'I don't think you have. You can just keep drawing.' She sits next to the girl and nods encouragingly during the drawing.

It is important to wait for the child's question. First, look closely at their face and body language: are they scared? Do they want something? Are they enjoying themselves? Based on that, you ask a question: Are you managing? What do you enjoy doing? Don't suggest something you've thought up too often, but rather let the child think about it. Give them the space to say yes or no to something or to come up with their own idea. People often forget to ask that kind of questions. They think they already know what a child needs.
Tihana Trputec, Altijd Lente Children's Centre, Amsterdam

Avoid making a judgement about the product, with older children too

Steering clear of judgements takes effort and can be difficult for adults. We're so used to doing it, it's almost a reflex. Especially when children ask for confirmation: 'Nice, isn't it?' – this makes sense, particularly if they are constantly being valued in this way. One way of dealing with this is to respond with another question: 'Are *you* satisfied with it? That is what I find important.'

Children may be surprised at first by your response, but you may notice them passing on your words later in the day to other children. Genuine interactions of this sort help to create a positive culture, where children can develop their confidence and steer clear of competition with each other. The more steadfast you are in being non-judgemental, the less children will seek approval and the more they will learn to trust their own opinions. This can take time but will be worth it to move away from the false culture of 'nice'.

The older a child gets, the more aware they will become of the values around them. This can lead to a perfectionist attitude. Giving the perfectionist child the confidence to create their own image of the world falls within the advanced art of a studio educator.

The key is *always* to focus on the process and stay away from compliments, such as 'well done', 'beautiful', 'great' and so on. This is particularly so with older children; judgement does not fit with discovery learning. Older children are excellent researchers and in this, there is only the experience. For example, something that is surprising, remarkable, intriguing, weird, exciting or, perhaps, relaxing, smooth, soft, rough or bumpy, wet or slimy, scary, cute or tasty – it is never right or wrong. Even if older children *do* start off with a plan or an idea of how something might turn out, there is still no need for judgement on your part. They may or may not reach an approximation of their goal – judgement has no place here. More valid: is the maker satisfied with it? Making reference to Arno Stern's rule – 'You don't comment on other people's work' – is *particularly* valuable with older children and is worth discussing with them.

Frustration in children

Frustrated children deserve our support. These are the children for whom something does not work straightaway, or who think they can't do something. You will enable these children, not by ignoring the difficulties or taking over the task, but by supporting them emotionally.

> Pleasure and difficulty come together in a learning process.
> Loris Malaguzzi

'Will you draw it for me?'

What do we do when children ask: 'I can't do that, will you draw it for me?' Steer clear of demonstrating for them, but do encourage them to visualise an image of whatever it is they want to draw. Help them with sensitive questions and small steps. For example, if they want to draw an elephant, you might expand on this thoughtfully, by asking: 'I wonder if it is big or small, or how many legs might it have? I wonder how we might recognise an elephant?'. A great way to begin a drawing is to build it up using the basic shapes (see IMG 2.4b, Section 2.1.2).

> It doesn't have to look like something to still be something.
> Titia Sprey

A circle can be used to symbolise a great many things. Reassure the child, their work does not have to be an exact copy of something, it is still valid and worthwhile however it looks and turns out.

Avoid letting children judge each other's work.

> If something doesn't work first time, encourage children to have another go. Similar to learning to walk, when you fall, you just have to get up and try again. Sometimes, it's a question of changing one line to make things right. A child needs contact and support for that. Sympathise with the child's frustration and offer not solutions but understanding. Encourage them to start again. That's the art and to do that, you have to know the child. It's important in that situation to literally stay close to the child and not give up; stick with it and feel almost as frustrated until it's over.
> Eve Rennebart, Atelier Turmalin, Berlijn

Beware of showing how to draw something: this can provoke an unequal relationship with the child. However, exceptions prove the rule: if you do decide to demonstrate, perhaps because the child has a concrete problem and has asked for help explicitly, then make a point of drawing on your own piece of paper and let the child draw on theirs. Most of all, encourage children to support each other, again each using their own piece of paper. That way, they build their relationships and develop learning.

By standing side by side with a child you will be an ally. The only way they will learn is if they experience for themselves how things work. We create an atmosphere of equivalence by sharing their curiosity. What do they discover? What do they need if they want to know, or do more? This kind of process only works if the adult steps back from imposing their image of the world on children in advance. Support children to find things out for themselves, either independently, or respectfully encourage children's own discussions with each other. And if there are questions or problems, by asking about possibilities they can come up with themselves.

Maintaining boundaries

Although working with the *Understanding Through Your Hands* approach means following the children's marks and initiatives, it does not mean that anything goes. In fact, nurturing children in their creative process is only doable with clear boundaries. This is one of the most difficult aspects, how best to formulate both rules for working, alongside your personal boundaries. The ability to indicate personal boundaries on time is therefore also a learning process for many adults.

> We sometimes come across a child whose behaviour isn't going well. What do you do in that situation? We talk about this a lot. What's the Reggio Emilia approach? Or do you just have to be authoritarian, by way of preserving the peace, before starting up the creative process again? There's a bit of friction there.
> Karin Voogt, Max Childcare, Rotterdam

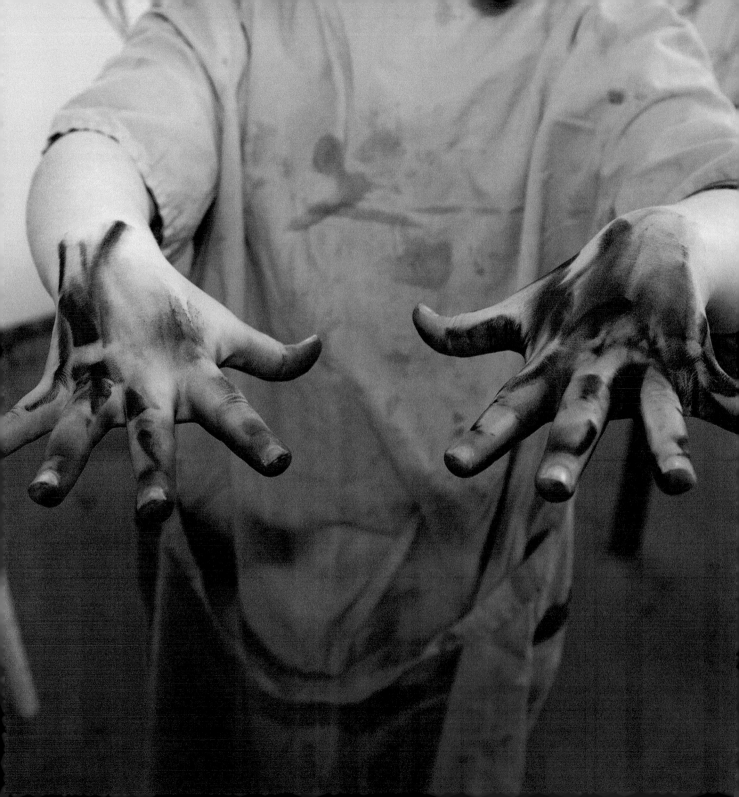

Personal boundary

Before you can set boundaries for children's behaviour, you must first know where your own lie. Identifying your personal boundaries and practising how to make others aware of them is something you continue to learn through life. In this context it is good to recognise that the more personally you formulate a boundary – *I don't want* things to be thrown around' – the better the child will understand (Juul, 1995).

Jesper Juul says that we want to give our children lots of space by raising them in a democratic and, consequently, more or less anti-authoritarian way. But adults still need to build their own authority, and this can take some searching. One way to do this is to indicate your boundary with personal authority: 'I don't want you to walk around with scissors, I am afraid you will fall and hurt yourself.' Not everything is allowed. You might hear adults say: 'Yes, sometimes you have to shout to establish order – then you just have to be authoritarian'. However, boundaries can also be established with clarity, and in ways that aren't hurtful. Interactions can involve both equivalence *and* clear consequences for behaviour. It is the educator's task *and* responsibility to devise positive and inviting situations for children. These will be framed by clear rules and mutual respect, *also* where there's conflict.

It's a kind of tipping point. Suddenly, it's there and nothing nice is happening anymore. It's being annoying for the sake of being annoying. Yelling and throwing things around. One minute they're concentrating on work, boisterous but enthusiastic, and the next, it's chaos. If I have the feeling that we're approaching such a turning point, I try to anticipate it. By taking a brief time-out. By letting them show each other all the things they're inventing, discovering and doing. If they're allowed to talk about that, it becomes very important again. They see what the others are doing and later, they calm down. You don't have to be strict to achieve that. There's just a quiet break. That's a positive thing whereas if you're strict, that's often negative. That tipping point frequently gets closer because one or two children are already nearly finished. That makes them restless.

Sanne Groen, Westerdok Children's Centre, Amsterdam

IMG. 3.37   After a long time concentrating on a painting session, a child covers their fingers in charcoal. The art
<   teacher makes no negative remarks. She sees that the children have finished drawing. It means that it is
             time to stop and go out into the garden to capitalise on the discoveries they've made.

IMG. 3.38   Help! I'm not always aware that my boundary is about to be reached. At a certain moment, I think: 'This is not fun anymore, help!'. Treating material without respect is one such boundary. You mustn't break things, like pencils being snapped in two, or grabbing for the sake of grabbing also irritates me.
Ingrid Veldman, Villa Petit Paradis Daycare Centre, Meppel

It's good to learn to see the difference between creative and destructive chaos. The former is necessary and the latter has to be avoided or turned around.

Apply golden rules and maintain your boundaries

Always approach children positively. That means saying what you do want or expect, rather than what you don't want. If they appear to be talking a lot, leave out any judgements about them being too boisterous, and calmly invite them to focus on what they are doing. Refer to the two golden rules – respect for the materials, and respect for each other. It is not a problem if a child does not want to join in, but the other children must not be disturbed.

Chaos and material

Chaos has to do with your boundaries, but also sometimes with the amount and variety of materials you are offering. Start simply, with small amounts of

IMG. 3.39   This child is busy writing on an envelope. She is talking to the adult about sending letters. She says she doesn't want to put her letter in the 'pretend letterbox' at the childcare centre; she wants to put in the real one, out in the street. She watches intently as the adult writes an address on the envelope.

dry materials in small dishes and gradually expand on this (crescendo-principle), or by combining things with water, glue, paint or clay.

Sharing technical knowledge

Early explorations using *all* of the senses is paramount. This gives children valuable opportunities to make marks and research the materials. There is no point in trying to teach technical knowledge whilst they are still in this exploratory phase; they won't be receptive to it. Restraint about techniques at this stage has several advantages: children familiarise themselves with the characteristics of the materials, and adults get the chance to see how receptive children are to them.

It is best to talk about technique after this exploration phase; the children will be open to this, and may even ask explicitly. In the latter, you might clearly demonstrate something, perhaps for the whole group. Through a desire to show something new or exciting, it is less likely to be a lecture, but more of a feeling of sharing knowledge.

Sharing technical knowledge is an important task for the studio educator but it is not the only goal. Personal understanding and experience of the materials is the key to offering children the right resources, in line with their interests – this will intensify their explorations.

IMG. 3.40   First give the children A6 cards and a few markers. Then, in-between times, jot down a comment in the notebook lying ready; that way, you're working too, and not looking over the children's shoulders.

3.2.5   Being witness to the creative process

As a studio educator, you witness the children's concentration. You know how a drawing or a scribbled drawing was created, or what a child told you about their clay work. You know the story behind what they have made. Writing down what the child says and has discovered is valuable because it is easy to forget exactly what happened and what the child has described. Making notes and working them out later takes time, it's true, but it's an important task.

Record in word and/or image
When we witness creative experiences, this places the emphasis on the process and not on the end result. Recording observations and the children's authentic comments makes it possible to go into the work in more depth. In this way, you transcend more general comments such as: 'They had great fun playing in the mud'. Clear notes on the significant points of play, mean you can find out exactly what they were doing and which associations they had while making mud.

There are three reasons why it's so valuable to record what you see and hear.
1   *Reflection and a reminder for yourself*
    You look back: what actually happened and why? And then: how can I elaborate, augment, go into more depth, or avoid or resolve the situation next time? This is the basis for new ideas and more intensity.

IMG. 3.41   If you only look superficially at this scribbling boy holding the marker in his fist, it is easy to overlook the amount of concentration and versatility of his work. To the left, you see a sketch book with a series of figures made by the same boy.

2   *Information and reflection with other adults*
Adults who work creatively with children can learn a lot from each other. Talking about practice, looking at photos or the things that children have made, can promote involvement and the sharing of ideas. Parents can also share in this process and will delight in seeing images, films or written observations of their children.

3   *For the children themselves*
Recording what children do and say means that you appreciate them. Looking back is also a reminder for them (where did we stop?) and also a possible starting point for more depth, repetition or a subsequent idea (where are we heading?).

Adults will sometimes report that they are too busy to document things. It can be helpful to think in *crescendo*, from small to large, and make notes during a creative activity or jot down what has happened discreetly in pencil below a drawing. That way, you don't need extra time to work out the notes. Once mastered, these short reports can be elaborated on, for example, by combining text with photos, or making short films or posts on social media.

Presenting
Let the children's visual language be seen in the spaces they live in, at school and at home. Display their drawings and paintings. Present authentic comments

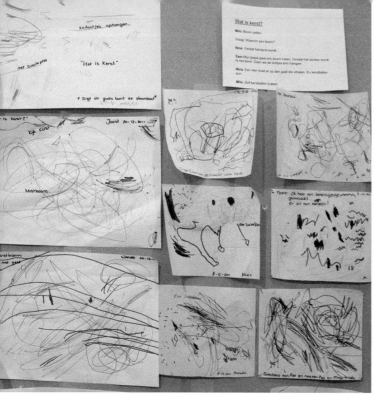

and describe their activities with short texts or illustrated notes in full view on the wall or in a book. If this is done regularly, a little at a time, documentation will grow of its own accord.

Importance of documentation

It demonstrates to children that you value their work when it is presented thoughtfully. A permanent documentation wall, preferably with a display cabinet, will allow you to rotate and change the children's discoveries on show. Photographs will make visible the layered nature of the creative process. Writing or printing some of the children's comments and/or a couple of 'wow' moments, will enrich the documentation, and add extra significance to the exhibits.

3.3   What the experts say

In this section, through exchanges with specialists, parents, host parents, educators and teachers you can see which approaches are used, based on different choice of materials and from a sound educational vision. It's not just about copying handicrafts, but about discovering, experimenting and children being allowed to shape their own ideas. See why and how you can focus on the process of discovery instead of on a nice or artistic product. The subject teachers in this section either consciously work without a theme, based on the material, or they work with a theme as an inspiring starting point, but leave scope for the children's own input.

3.3.1   *Titia Sprey, studio educator, Kris Kras Studio, Amsterdam*

In my Kris Kras Studio there are always 3 or 4 workstations next to each other. One offers drawing in a small format, one offers construction, or a specific technique, and another offers free play. Children may choose where they start and switch stations if they wish. What is offered changes every week, but always has materials that invite mark-making and research. The appealing aspect is in the material itself, but also in the way I lay it out, the *prepared environment*. For example, at a drawing table, I lay out an A6 card for each child, with a black pen, two coloured felt-tipped pens, a hole punch or herb scissors, or an old-fashioned slide rule. The tables are set with care, a bit like in a restaurant, so that you really want to sit down and taste. I don't lay out too many things at the same time, so that the children can focus well.

The free play station doesn't need much supervision, which allows me to give the other stations more of my attention. The attraction of the material at the free play station is so strong that the children dive into it of their own accord. It could be a large, shallow container filled with, for example, flour or lentils, or wooden rings or lids. This is presented in as tempting a way as possible. This type of material is just as popular with infants from 18 months, as it is with older children up to 10 years.

IMG. 3.42   From top left to right: the practitioner has typed out a conversation about Christmas and hung it with
<   the children's drawings on the subject. Next to that: the studio educator is observing the children and noting down comments in a small notebook. These will be combined with photos later, and after the display comes down, they will be filed in an A4 folder. From bottom left to right: A clothes hanger for trousers is handy for collecting a pile of paintings. It invites you to leaf through the paintings and saves space. Next to this, the drawings have been bound together with a clasp keyring to make a personal, mark-making book.

I always keep material and/or tools hidden to support and deepen the children's concentration later on in the process. The materials often are everyday objects, found in recycling shops, the DIY store or supermarket. You won't find glitter in my studio, but you will find flour shakers! Playing with foodstuffs is safe and enjoyable for children, and it provides fulfilling learning experiences. I am sometimes asked about sustainability. I believe this material is more sustainable than glitters or plastic. I share a bucket of 5 kilos of orange lentils with four colleagues. For the past 10 years, more than 500 children have played with it. It is important to clean the floor before putting it out, so the lentils can be reused over and over again.

In order to shorten preparation and clearing-up time, 3 groups of 8 come during the studio day. The children aged between 18 months and 4 years attend with their parents in the morning, and those that attend in the afternoon are aged 4 years and up. I stick to the same workstations for a day, in principle. I may adjust several things for the older children, aged 8 plus. For example, there might be a glue gun and containers of assorted plastic with which they can work with independently. In a way, this is also a kind of free-play station.

A very important characteristic of the Kris Kras Studio is that the children have the freedom to make what they want. There is never an assignment or a theme. Recently, one child said: 'Everyone who knows you, Titia, knows that you never tell them what they have to make; with you, we can always choose ourselves. That's much more fun!' My approach is to support the children to follow their ideas. In that way, they find out what they like, and discover what they want and how to get there. Then the ideas really start to flow. I facilitate this through observing, tuning into what is needed and respond to this. My aim is always to do this as unobtrusively as possible – this allows the children to carry on undisturbed, though aware that they have been noticed. The biggest compliment is if a child says: 'Ah, that's exactly what I need!'.

Importance of an inner compass

Children who choose their own direction learn to respond to their feelings. They build an *inner compass* in this way. And that's something we sorely need in the world. In the current education system, children, generally, are expected to follow and comply with a teacher's directions. Contrary to this, I believe in the value of maintaining and developing a connection to the inner self. That way, children learn to trust in their own judgement and abilities. If you facilitate children during their research, this enables a state of flow; a natural optimum state of learning – in other words, they're playing.

The children might not know what they are doing at first, but begin by making marks. Then there is the power of imagination, or an image or an idea. All of which can change during the process. That is *Understanding Through Your Hands;* there is usually no planning beforehand – the key is to be led by your own marks. This is sometimes a challenge for adults who prefer to know first what the result will be. There may already be expectations; what will it be, what are

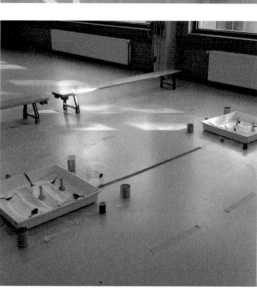

you making? But the children are at the initial phase of discovering, learning to make their own choices and gaining valuable experience: what does this material do, how does it work? These multi-sensory activities build and strengthen connections in the brain, forming a web of knowledge, as children learn through play, art and science.

The Kris Kras Studio is not there to train children to be visual artists. Rather, it offers a rich creative experience, where children learn by experimenting, similar to the strategies used by artists and scientists. Freedom of choice leads to intrinsic motivation, the driver for developing a range of valuable skills, including both fine and gross motor, and social and emotional competences.

As an artist educator, I am witness to the creative process. I document the comments and actions of children to illustrate how they arrive at their discoveries. In the case of the youngest children, I ask the parents to do this. It is not always clear which processes lead to a particular outcome. In many cases, there is no permanent product, as in the play with lentils. The benefits are within the child's thinking, it could be said that the true documentation is always in the child's mind. Literally: 10,000 scribbles equal 10,000 neural connections.

IMG. 3.43 A prepared environment invites the children to play and research. There are always a number of
<   different workstations in the Kris Kras Studio. This includes a 'free play station', often with a large
             container full of one kind of material, such as flour or red lentils. Here, there is one in a school gym
             (middle photo). Materials and tools are laid out as attractively and clearly as possible to invite curiosity
             and the children's urge to begin.

IMG. 3.44 Children are allowed to choose for themselves what they want to do and make; there are no themes or
>   assignments in the Kris Kras Studio. This allows for authentic images. When children are working, every
             so often they will spontaneously tell you about it. A studio educator can encourage these interactions
             by asking open questions. From top left to right, Photo 1: Minecraft, natural clay with little pieces cut
             from chicken wire (boy, 8 years old). Photo 2: 'Pete on a hill with a gate', recycled material with glue
             gun (boy, 11 years old). Photo 3: 'A ginger tomcat, with wool of course' (girl, 8 years old). From middle
             left to right, Photo 4: 'A line out for a walk', Ecoline (boy, 5 years old). Photo 5: 'Santa Claus with a
             nosebleed', salt dough and felt-tipped pen (boy, 5 years old). Photo 6: 'Herring gull', permanent marker
             (boy, 6 years old). From bottom left to right, Photo 7: 'Castle', cardboard and recycled material with
             glue gun (girl, 7 years old). Photo 8: 'Coach and horses', Styrofoam board with screws (girl, 8 years old).
             Photo 9: 'A little owl', natural clay with feathers (boy, 8 years old).

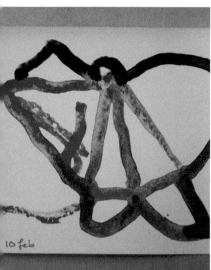

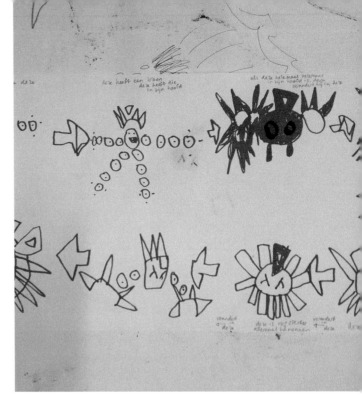

IMG. 3.45   A boy at the Kris Kras Studio makes a print by carefully pressing a thin sheet onto his wet painting and drawing on it with a stick.

3.3.2 Heidi de Geus, studio educator, BouwWerk lessons, De Bron Primary School, Amsterdam

I am a subject teacher and an artist educator, and I give lessons in art and design (BouwWerk) at De Bron Primary School where I have my own classroom, set up as a studio. I teach children from 4 to 12 years old. There was a need for visual arts lessons at that school, with the focus on spatial design.

With my BouwWerk lessons, I try to tap into the children's fantasy and powers of imagination and give them full rein. It's all about them being able to make discoveries, come up with solutions and shape and design their own ideas. That way, they learn through play to work with a variety of materials and the accompanying techniques. We often work with no-cost materials collected by parents, such as egg boxes, cardboard, plastic bottles and cups, caps and corrugated cardboard. All ideal material for researching and making connections.

The children are all enthusiastic when we work with river clay. I take photos of their studies and we use the photos in the next lesson to discuss which techniques they used: you can make something by removing material, by sticking it together or by reshaping it.

I also really like to use insulation wire (plastic-covered copper wire). It's quite easy to bend and cut, but you can still make solid shapes with it. For example, I once gave children a research assignment which was to make a shape that could stand on its own. This wire figure can later be clad with modelling wax.

In my lessons, I focus on learning through research and process. The idea is that research → leads to creating → which leads to reflection (and collaboration, working autonomously and presenting). And you can actually see these competencies developing in the children. The great thing about this way of working is that it's all about how children work and not about what exactly they're going to make. For me, the end result is secondary to the process, although naturally the children do try to make a really cool piece of work, something they're proud of. I've noticed that the feeling of pride is greatest when they've been able to make something all by themselves.

Ownership

We work on one essential element in these lessons: ownership. It means that learning only becomes significant when the children's own interests are addressed. So, I pay extra attention to the children's initiatives and to small, unexpected things. I also find it important that they are able to create without judgement from others. If they ask me if something is beautiful, I say: 'It's not important what I think of your work, I want to know what you think of it'. How the class teacher and I do this in practice is a fascinating quest, and a recurring learning process since our opinions sometimes differ. It's trial and error.

Adults have a facilitating and supporting role in the BouwWerk lessons. This entails, for example, holding the paper while a child cuts it, though not cutting it for

---

IMG. 3.46 << Top photos: This boy likes to draw on the floor at the Kris Kras Studio. The drawing takes on significance for others when you add his comments (with respect for the work itself, in pencil and in small letters).

IMG. 3.47 << Bottom photos: By giving children real material and good tools, you take them seriously in their creative research. And if you supervise that attentively, you can actually start them at a young age, like this 2-year-old boy at the Kris Kras Studio.

IMG. 3.48 > During the BouwWerk lesson: constructing with insulation wire, various no-cost materials, wood and coloured sticky tape. Artist Alexander Calder was the source of inspiration. The research assignment for children during the construction work is 'Make something hover'. This invites children to carefully consider the possibilities the material offers. There are various possible solutions. Photo 1 (from left to right): Boy working on his project, concentrated and in flow. Photo 4: Exposition of the work in the auditorium: construction with drawing.

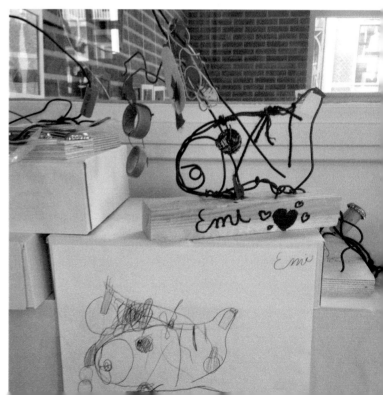

IMG. 3.49   A poster for the BouwWerk lesson, where Alexander Calder was the source of inspiration, at an exhibition in the auditorium. At the bottom, the descriptions of the research assignments: * Try to draw (in your sketch book) with 1 line, * Experiment with the black thread, * Attach everything securely, * Make something hover, * Draw what you've constructed.

them. Also, by asking the right questions, we can help children solve problems by themselves. For example, a child says that their piece of work keeps falling over. In that case, I ask: 'Why do you think that's happening? What could you do to make it stronger/straighten it up/ make it steadier?'. You can look at it this way: we assist children with their projects. They take the initiative and can ask us for help or assistance.

I often take an artist as starting point or inspiration for my lessons. We look together at a piece of art on the interactive whiteboard. I then ask the question: 'What's happening here?'. I've taken that from VTS (Visual Thinking Strategies) which is a teaching method that works with open questions on art. It's important to me that everyone can take part in looking at art. And it's not about what you know, it's about what you see and what it says to you. Plus, children learn to listen attentively to each other and to look carefully at details.

Each schoolyear, the children are given a 'research book', a blank notebook. They make drawing games in it and stick pictures of art works in, that they later draw. The drawing games are a good way of letting go of the idea that you can't draw, or for when you don't know what you want to draw. The emphasis is on pleasure, surprising yourself and getting ideas from looking at what appears on your paper. You can use that to take things further. Lastly, the children also draw their own pieces of work which is a nice, calm way of reflecting. The research book helps to make learning visible both for the pupil and the teacher.

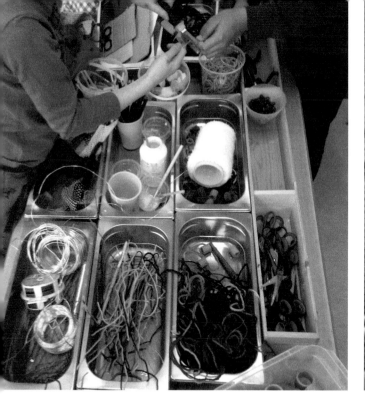 

IMG. 3.50   Photo left: various construction and connecting materials and tools arranged and laid out clearly. Photo right: a tortoise made of open-ended waste material around the theme of plastic soup/global warming.

I start my lessons with an explanation about materials, tools and any necessary announcements. I do that in the children's own classroom. We then go the studio, already set out, so that the children can get to work immediately. I try to present everything to be as inviting as possible; the materials are sorted into containers on the table, the tools are lying ready on the woodwork table. I always have some new material to hand in order to refresh the attention and focus after a while.

The first lesson is generally aimed at materials research, sometimes with a research question for more detail, such as: how do you connect materials without glue or sticky tape? Or: how do you make a tower that can stand alone? Only after that first lesson do I think about what the following lessons should be. Sometimes, certain material turns out to evoke something completely different in the children than I had expected. I once offered them bits of coloured filter during a lesson in which they could make lanterns. Almost the whole group abandoned the lanterns and focused on making glasses instead! I find it important to leave space for this kind of initiative and I enjoy it too. The children amaze me time and again with their discoveries and ideas. Expect the unexpected!

I work with the whole class, sometimes 30 children at a time. In that case, it's impossible to follow all individual processes and respond to them. It's lovely to see that children often help, inspire and learn from each other.

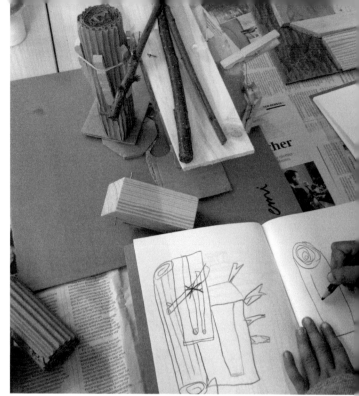

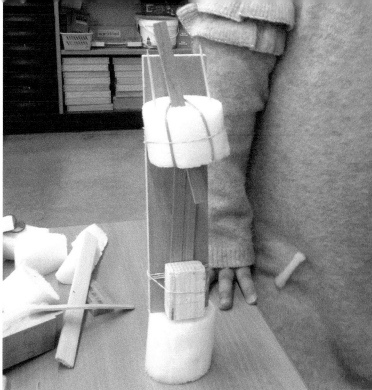

IMG. 3.52   Materials research with no-cost materials. How do you build a tower without glue, sticky tape or nails?

Because I take so many photos, I sometimes gain insight afterwards into the strategies the children use in their work. And when they write something about their work during the last lessons – that tells me a lot too. I try to take some time with their teacher to discuss anything we noticed during the lesson. Sometimes, a child will have struggled enormously with the material, the technique or themselves. Sometimes, someone has had to overcome something during the lessons, maybe without a tangible end result but with a new learning moment gained. Those are important observations for me and for the teacher.

3.3.3 Sanne Groen, artist at children's centres and schools

I get ideas by talking to the pedagogic staff or by just walking around the supermarket. From the things I buy for myself in particular, I get lots of ideas. I work a lot with sensory experiences. That has everything to

IMG. 3.51   BouwWerk lesson by Heidi de Geus: Drawings in the research book of the construction made as part of
<   the reflection on their own work. Photo 1 (top left): a drawing of a sculpted shape of aluminium foil in
            the research book as drawing game, warm-up. Photo 3 (bottom right): a drawing in the research book
            of a work of art, practice for learning to observe well.

do with feeling, smelling, pouring and mixing. Mixing things together, experimenting and researching, both the children and I really enjoy that.

I also often take the weather into consideration. If it's very sunny, I try to make use of the sunlight with the shadow, colours and transparency. If it's raining, we collect the water and use it. Or we make something in the puddles with leaves, a flower or some colour. And now it's getting colder, I'm thinking about all the things we can do with cold things, with ice and melting.

I think I just look really carefully at what happens at the beginning. One child wants to touch something, another takes a spoon or tweezers. Age doesn't make much difference; I work a lot with babies. I can spend *hours* doing that – it is such fun. I hadn't expected that because you demand a lot of concentration and at first, you don't think they can do that. Yes, it's always a mess in the end! But that's my trademark. In terms of energy, I have various groups. I think up something different for a boisterous group than for a quiet one. I don't like assignments – they are much too restrictive. You can do more difficult things with older children,

drawing perspective for example, but you offer that at the moment they're interested in it.

Naturally, drawing is wonderful. Both boys and girls can really enjoy drawing. It's great. I'm not a fan of colouring books because they mean the children don't have to come up with ideas themselves. Colouring books are just about staying inside the lines. But a blank sheet of paper can become anything at all. Left to their own devices, children make truly authentic drawings. Much more interesting than those in a colouring book.

You always have one or two children who are less interested. Sometimes they find it too much commotion. At the table, I watch what happens when I give them other things, without saying too much. Often, they'll get to work after all. And sometimes, they don't want to and that's fine too. Not wanting to join in due to fear of the unknown is not the same as not wanting to join in because they think they can't do it.

I involve the pedagogic staff a lot. They see what happens and can continue the process in the children's care. I often leave little things behind for them to use.

IMG. 3.53   Sanne Groen presents the children with aromatic herbs and liquids. She lays out test tubes, pipettes,
>   funnels and jars. Some children are hesitant, others get right down to researching. Children watch a lot
             of what someone else is doing, and give each other ideas. At a certain moment they are in flow and
             forget everything else around them.

IMG. 3.54   If children are given challenging material, you're surprised how well they master their fine motor skills. This 2-year-old boy is moving very small material from one jar to another using tweezers.

When they're here, the pedagogic staff sometimes ask the children questions like 'What are you making?', *just* as they're engrossed in their activity. But it's difficult to find the right balance between saying nothing and asking the right questions. I sometimes have to help the staff with allowing a mess to be made. Something falls to the floor and you hear their shock: 'Oh!'. And then I say: 'That's lovely, look at them go, I wonder what they're going to do with that!'. That's a different approach. I don't see a mess; I see children enjoying themselves. Some children spill water as they're pouring but I think that's great, that not all the water fits in the tube, and that they experience that too. Look at that girl rubbing her hand through the water: 'I'm making it awaaaay,' she said. I find not making a mess *so* restrictive.

I mostly take the material as my starting point. For example, I have aromatics. Then I think that it would be nice to introduce those tweezers and test tubes with them. I'm curious to see what will happen then. Later, all sort of things are added: colour, or flavours.

Corn or potato starch is nice material, and I also make salt bread dough with food colouring. That has a nice feel to it. And blancmange, that's also all about feeling.

Sometimes I combine it with hot and cold. And with sounds; something that rustles. Or with something that lets light through. That can be anything. For example, with gelatine leaves it's extra beautiful, because there are air bubbles in them. And if you make them wet, they become soft. It breaks really easily but if it's wet, you can also tear it. And it becomes paint, because it releases its colour. Then you see really lovely things. You can make coloured shadows on the ground with it.

> **Simple purchase of materials**
> I mostly buy materials in the supermarket, at the wholesaler or on the Internet. I bought wooden materials and those little spoons there too. They have a lot of packaging materials. Plus, I have all sorts of tools – tubes and jars, sticky tape and wire. Nothing pre-processed. No patterns or templates. Sometimes, I find material: these little wooden bars for the test tubes were a find, and I bored holes in them with a thick drill.

With the babies, I sometimes work with fruit, which we smash. With slightly older children, we add a bit of flour and red cabbage or beetroot, blackberries, flowers… I once added bicarbonate of soda and vinegar and that effervesces – real magic. And if you also put a bit of soap in – but you mustn't do that with really young children – it overflows. It's fun with red cabbage because a little bit of soda turns it green. Vinegar turns it bright red and bicarbonate of soda turns it blue. It's like chemistry, I love it. I don't add soda if I'm working with very young children. And I never say beforehand what will or could happen; it's much more fun if they discover that for themselves.

3.3.4 Mirja van der Bijl, studio educator, Laterna Magica Children's Centre, Amsterdam

We are an integrated centre for children aged 0 to 12 years and we have more than 800 pupils. It's an exceptional school which has a central area, dedicated to learning through discovery. Our vision on learning entails taking natural learning as a premise: we see children's enquiring minds as a resource. Here, children discover how something is created or how it works. They gain new knowledge and as they do, they develop skills and insights. Children also learn by listening to, playing and working with other children. Our rich learning environment is still developing. We now have a discovery garden, vegetable garden, radio studio, kitchen, outdoor workstation, spa and art library. As coaches and professionals, we form a teaching landscape in which we reflect and design together and commit to an authentic learning environment for children.

Young children fascinate me. That's partly due to the exhibition 'The Children of Reggio Emilia' in the Stedelijk Museum in Amsterdam in 1996. I was so impressed. You were given a peek into the wealth of their research, a true argument for the imaginative powers of young children. How was it possible that we adults had so little faith in the potential that children are born with? In addition to the inspiration from Reggio Emilia, I also apply the *Understanding Through Your Hands* approach which revolves around basing your thinking on material. There is no assignment or theme, only a prepared environment which invites children to get to work, often non-verbally. That means there is no pressure because something has to be done, an aspect that older

children sometimes appreciate too. Through research, trial and error and play, it's possible that something can be created. In that case, you are surprised by your own process.

I give children the tranquillity and space to get researching. Naturally, it all starts with material that piques their curiosity and invites endless transformation. How you offer and introduce the material is also important. For example, with natural clay, we start with a ritual of waking and warming up our hands. It's very simple, but it gets us focusing on what we're going to do. And that's when the art of watching and listening starts for me. What are the children doing, what do they need, what are they interested in, what are they communicating? That can be verbal but more often, it's non-verbal. That's how I see how the children learn in their own way. As adults, we're used to often working towards a goal, to taking the shortest route from A to B. Consequently, we don't take the time to watch exactly what a child is researching and where they digress to. And precisely those digressions are the source of creativity.

Go off the beaten track in your brain!
The creative activities in our current handicrafts culture consist mainly of predetermined assignments aimed at an end product. We've all seen that classroom with 25 stereotyped products on the wall, so similar that the children often wonder which one is their own. In the *Understanding Through Your Hands* way of working, the focus is on a wide selection of open-ended materials that get processes going. Children feel they're being

invited to research and to play. The focus is on children's creative processes rather than on the end product and if there is an end product, it reveals the child's individuality.

I believe we should let go of the idea of end products thought up by adults.

The main task of the adult is to give a child space to collect intense experiences. I take the individuality and research of every child seriously. Consequently, every child feels they have been seen. That means they can apply their talents to give meaning to the world. Building their own knowledge. And researching, playing, learning and concentrating all go hand in hand with that. Yesterday, a girl aged two and a half spent an hour with natural clay and a small water sprayer. While spraying, she became completely engrossed in rubbing the clay which was becoming increasingly smooth. Without saying anything, I gave her a spoon. She took the spoon and made endless rubbing movements with the back of the spoon to smooth the clay. She then sprayed drops of water very meticulously on each of her fingers and rubbed that into the wet clay. She did that for an hour. You see flow occurring: she and her research were one.

Children should always be able to draw based on their own strengths and imagination, not on being shown how. In my studio, I let children from the age

IMG. 3.55   *Children drawing in the garden of Laterna Magica.*

<

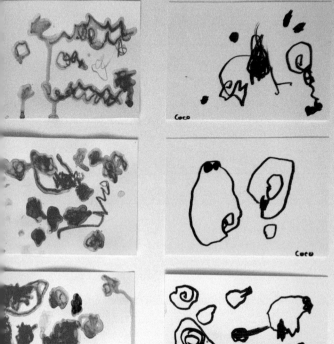

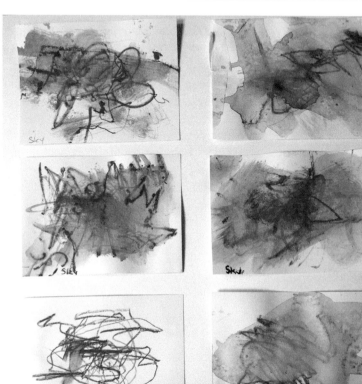

of 18 months research how you can draw and scribble with various materials; with mud, water, chalk or combinations of those. Everything they make goes into their A6 format 'marks book'. Scribbling is fun, it's how everyone starts drawing. It's so many things at once: making marks, an extension of your body, energy, release – it doesn't have to have a goal, that's the great thing about it. So, every book of marks illustrates a journey of discovery, observation and form. More and more, throughout the 3 years that the children's books get fuller, you see each child developing their own handwriting.

At Laterna Magica, we have a discovery garden for the youngest children and one for older children. I often go there exploring first with the children before going back to the studio. Recently, they got interested in spiders. We saw a big spider's web and a spider, hidden behind a leaf. One child touched it and another wanted to feed it grass. One 3-year-old said: 'Spiders eat insects, not grass'. After a short chat about that, we started drawing, outdoors, close to the spider's web (see IMG. 3.55). I consciously didn't tell them to draw a spider, but it's always an enriching experience to draw outdoors. Their scribbles and drawings were all different, but they all had the shape of a spider's web. Some had a black spot – the spider maybe? It's really special being able to see how the drawings reflect their sharpened observation skills.

We are born with enquiring minds. Curiosity is a powerful talent with which to get to know the world, through discovery. When children are occupied with something based on their own interest, a high degree of involvement, focus and concentration occurs.

By experimenting with materials, associating, playing, researching and philosophizing, you create neural pathways in your brain. The more pathways, the more creatively you are able to think, connect, feel and learn.

It's our task, as adults, to give children time to do their own research, to trust in their own creative ability – a trust that is based on equivalence and mutual respect.

3.3.5 Ank Bredewold, art teacher, Het Gein Primary School, Amsterdam Zuidoost

I have 2 ways of working: small groups of 8 children, as in my theatre group, and a classroom situation. In the classroom situation, the class teacher is always present for the social element. I am there for the visual arts input. What I always try to do is have the children

IMG. 3.56
<<
Children in concentration: understanding through their hands. Photo 4: Mirja van der Bijl took some mirrors into the garden, 'to see what the sky looks like today. What colour do you see? What is happening with the clouds?' She laid the mirrors on the grass and asked: 'What's it like seeing the sky on the ground?' One girl crawled across the mirrors and said: 'Look, I'm walking on the clouds now!'.

IMG. 3.57
<
Top: children's mark-making books in the studio of Mirja. Bottom: a number of A6 cards showing two children's own research.

research on their own, find things out for themselves. In the regular curriculum too. If there are 18 children in the class, they will not produce 18 frogs that are the same.

Children can contribute far more input than you might think. If you say that they're allowed to draw for themselves, teachers then give them blank sheets of paper and tell them to get on with it. As long as they're happily occupied. The children will then draw either the same horse every time or a racing car but that will be the end of it. In a classroom, I constantly walk the same route past them; if it's a small group, they come to me of their own accord. I look, I help them, and I talk to them. If there's something important, I point that out to the whole group. That way, they actually learn something, which I find important. They're learning through discovery, but it helps if you keep giving them impetus. That might consist of explaining what a horizon is if they're drawing a landscape. If you look at the horizon, what do you see? Is it nearby or far away? What does the horizon actually mean? In conversations, you discover that they used to think the world ended at the horizon. So, if you're standing there, you think that the horizon is farther away again, so it never ends. That way, you take the children a step further than if you say nothing, or just: 'Not like that, like this'.

Correcting them in the sense of: 'The sky isn't green, it's blue', is pointless. Or if children ask: 'I can't draw a rabbit, will you draw it for me?'. Instead of that, I talk to them about how a child feels about that animal and what is typical of a rabbit – what sort of things it has. It's nice and soft – how could you draw that softness? Maybe you should start by drawing a pile of softness and then see if it has ears. Because ears are also a characteristic of rabbits. And that pile of softness – does it also have feet? Sometimes, we take a look at a picture of a rabbit.

I never give just one example, always a huge pile.

Because you then think: I don't remember, are those back legs really big, or not. I give examples of how artists regard images of animals, people or things. That way, the children see that it doesn't have to be photographic, that everyone has their own way of seeing things. I never give just one example, always a huge pile. I will have partially prepared that so I'll either have it lying ready or it will be ready on the interactive whiteboard, but an awful lot derives from what I come across.

Most of all, I want children to come in and say: 'We're going to make this or that, and I need that and that.' I always try to respond to what's happening in the class. If the oldest children are working on a project about the

IMG. 3.58   This girl gets started straight away, completely doing her own thing and getting ideas from the
>   material. And though there's commotion around her, she works on, undisturbed. She decorates her
                 work with a narrow, shiny ribbon. At the opening of the closing exhibition, she tells all the parents
                 what she has made.

Second World War, one of them will research having to hide while another will look into the armies or the food provisions. They are working cognitively on that for two weeks and then they think about what they're going to do in my lesson; that might be painting a triptych, making a diorama or costumes. Sometimes, the teacher has given me a list so that I know if I should lay out something special. That has gradually become the system through the years. It works perfectly for the oldest children. I find that integration important; it's also mentioned in our school's policy plan.

The size of the groups is no problem for me, I'm used to it. I built the sound machine that stays in the hallway with whole classes. They all did something different. They collected crazy materials that had to be connected. It was really big and disorderly, but I've rarely seen a lesson in which every child was so involved. Some classes have 28 children. One year, there were combination groups of 32 children, but that's impossible. So I worked with half the group. The disadvantage of that is that the class teacher isn't involved. They are working with the other half of the group so they can't be here. Normally, teachers are always involved.

It's important that children are helped the right way and that parents don't ask the wrong questions. That's why I gave the children a letter for their parents which tells them what they might ask and how they can respond to what a child brings home. Basically, you shouldn't even mention the word beautiful. It's my first impulse too, if a child makes something: that's beautiful! And then I think 'Oh stupid, you've said it again!'. These are the examples of the questions I mention in the letter to the parents:

How did you make it?

Which part did you enjoy most?

What is it made of?

Can you tell me something about it?

Have you ever done anything like this before?

What could you call your piece?

How did you start?

Did you work on it for long?

How did you come up with the idea?

I review the work with the children together, using the museum model. The children set out their pieces like a little exhibition and we pretend we're in a museum. Then you can go and look in the next space (= the next table). That way, they look at each other's work and write down suggestions and compliments on pieces of paper I have laid out especially. Suggestions are things like: 'You could have used red too', 'It would have been nice if you had also used another colour'. Compliments are for the things they think are good about the piece

IMG. 3.59 > These children use open-ended materials to make props for a film production: boxes, cloths, crown caps, flat cardboard and connecting materials such as needle and thread and sticky tape. They have been working on this project together for a number of weeks with pleasure and good focus.

and they say that too. And if the pieces are hung up in their own classroom, the comments are hung up with them. I take into account what children do in their class in other subjects and in the visual arts class. Both involve working with your head and your hands. That's just as cognitive a subject as all others. It happens here, in their brains, in the studio too. You have a different entry point than with the other subjects, but you're still undeniably working with the children using their brains. It's one of many forms of expression – it could also be a poem or singing something. There are hundreds of ways of expressing yourself.

What I find the most important of all, is that I want to stimulate the children's curiosity about what life is. Because I notice that children very rarely do handicrafts or play outside at home. They experiment and play far too little. After all, playing is the ultimate way to learn. They are bombarded with the digital world and there is much distraction: television and computer games. Sometimes, they go from one club to another. And in those clubs, there is always someone who determines what they'll do there – whether they jump high or low or kick a ball or not. The children don't have to think it up for themselves. And if there's a moment where they have nothing to do, they get bored because they're unable to think: 'What now?'.

It's vital that children are allowed to draw and paint at home. At the most, there are two children in a class who are allowed to do that; the other parents feel it makes too much mess. I notice that teachers also find 'learning through discovery' too vague. Teachers prefer to have something to hold on to: a booklet that says: Give children a piece of paper, 15 x 20, and chalk, and have them draw circles. That's how teachers most like

to give lessons. And after that 7-minute instruction, the children get to work and the teacher gets on with marking papers. Because that teacher doesn't realise that it's only *now* that it starts. Now you say, for example: 'You've made that circle small or big but what would happen if you let those circles overlap?'. Teachers don't often think of that. In some progressive teacher training, they're told that you shouldn't let the children make pre-determined products such as 20 of the same frogs, sunflowers or snowmen. But that's as far as it goes. They're not told what they should do instead. Or how to challenge the children.

3.4 Finding your own style of working with *Understanding Through Your Hands*

How you supervise children in creative activities is largely dependent on your own expectations and experience. Being personally creative evokes many emotions; 'I'm not creative' is something you often hear. But whether or not you consider yourself to be creative, it's actually about trusting the *children's* creative abilities.

> Don't let a child hear you say that you can't draw or that you're not creative. Our kids learn from what we model!
> Jean van't Hul

Look at the marks the children make, both in daily life and in the studio. Think about how you can support them or intensify the research with additional material. One mark leads to another; that's the key to flow, the ultimate state of learning.

> Why are we not getting the best out of people? Because we are raised primarily to be hard workers, not creative thinkers. Children's restless minds and bodies are stigmatised or ignored, instead of cultivated for their energy and curiosity. In time, we don't teach children to be creative but rather not to be creative.
> Sir Ken Robinson, cultural leader during a TED conference in 2006

From product-oriented to process-oriented

Don't take the end product as your starting point: '*What* are we going to make?' but start from 'Which material shall I put out?'. Provide a prepared environment and use open-ended materials that invite research and mark-making. It's better to restrict the materials you offer, suited to your target group, than to let children take everything out of the cupboard themselves. That way, you give a framework and provide focus. Creativity thrives from restrictions, in fact, and it makes things more feasible for you, the studio educator.

Basic workshops that can be provided

Children's creative processes are taken seriously by giving them good-quality tools like scissors and markers that work. Using neutral white rather than brightly coloured paper is part of that too. The basic selection needed for making marks fits into a shoebox: a pile of A6 cards, black pens, a few coloured markers, scissors, a hole punch and a roll of sticky tape. Another basic selection of *Understanding Through Your Hands* is working with salt bread dough or natural clay. The corresponding tools can be found in any kitchen drawer: breakfast knives (rounded tip), a cake server, garlic press, potato masher, corkscrew, rolling pin and wooden skewers.

IMG. 3.60
<
Find your own way of working: some like to offer 'wet' workshops with things like paint or glue. Others prefer 'dry' workshops, such as building with loose parts or research with an overhead projector, as seen here in the photo.

IMG. 3.61
>
From top left to right: Constance Bogers, Krinkelwinkel, The Hague: 'You have to be open to children in outside-school care. I actually let them do anything. Obviously, you have to stay alert and try to make contact. If they grab for things, I ask: "I think maybe other children will need some later too, don't you think?". I avoid saying that something is not allowed. I ask questions. If you do that, you get the answer you want. Leave room for an equivalent dialogue.' Next to that: studio educator Ursula Woerner collects all kinds of material from the city waste depot to use in children's centres. From bottom left to right: artist Ilse van Lieshout always has her guitar in her studio to let children see and hear that music is also a language. Next to that: Lenka Slivkova, Altijd Lente Children's Centre, Amsterdam 'If I occasionally have an off day, I come here and within five minutes, there's a smile on my face. It's always a pleasure.'

Having two different workstations – next to each other – works well. Next to a basic drawing table as mentioned above, you can offer a play station, such as a sandpit or container with lentils. *Or* you can offer a construction station in addition to the drawing table. For example a workstation with cardboard and wood glue, or with clothes pegs and spatulas. This gives children a choice and they can stay at one station for a short while, or longer, if they prefer. An alternating selection allows children to experience new things and become familiar and confident with techniques and materials previously offered.

A restrained but alert attitude

If the *Understanding Through Your Hands* approach is new to you, we recommend working with as little talk as possible to begin with. This will support you to develop your skills as an interested witness – 'speech is silver and silence is golden'. It is an excellent way to gain expertise, and to develop understanding of the sorts of interactions that will support the process, as opposed to more product-oriented compliments such as 'beautiful', which interrupt.

Focus on a prepared environment that is not too full. Keep materials and tools to one side, ready to be introduced later in small amounts. This can be done in silence. It is a way to prompt less confident children to have a go, and support the ones who shout 'I'm finished!' too soon, to persevere. A child who is tearing clay into small pieces can be given scissors or a container to put the pieces in. A child who has been drawing for some time already can simply be offered a new blank card. Young children are very capable of communicating whether they want something or not. They feel seen when the adult is attentive and attuned to their activity.

Doing it a lot and 'learning by doing'

Taking a position of equivalence in your interactions with children is an explicit, conscious attitude, that demands commitment and experience. It is not easy to hold back and give no instruction and no direction, and stop yourself from sharing your opinions of the world. It is a case of trial and error – learning by doing. Finding your own style of teaching and engaging in dialogue, requires practice – you do not find your style of working overnight!

If you are more familiar with giving assignments, you might find it easier to gradually offer children more freedom, so that you get used to this new way of working. If you usually begin with an example, give a number of examples from nature, by way of photos or objects. Rather than an exercise to copy, discuss with the children what they see. After that, allow them to choose the provocations and ideas that they are drawn to, or most interested in.

You can also let the children in a class draw freely on A6 cards or perhaps offer them their own drawing books to work in. Whilst they draw or scribble, you can read them a story or introduce a piece of music to listen to. This is really about mark-making, so there is *no* assignment. This could become a regular ritual, for example, each Monday morning, in a circle for 10 minutes. Children will appreciate this tradition.

You might do your own research on social media to see how others work with *Understanding Through Your Hands* (#understandingthroughyourhands and in Dutch: #begrijpenmetjehanden). What materials do they use, and which 'wow' moments do they document? What obstacles do they encounter and how can you learn from each other?

IMG. 3.62   With a restrained but alert attitude the studio educator is watching and enjoying how the boy discovers papier-maché, made from green egg cartons and water.

> Take pleasure in what you do; enjoying supporting children is the first priority. And, if you have that, you radiate it too. It is the source of all life. Clear your mind and at the same time, be alert.
> Dagmar Arzenbacher, Schuppen 9 training studio, Berlin

Lastly: learning from the children

You will always learn by being open and receptive to children. This will also involve tuning in to their positive and negative responses. Both are legitimate reactions, depending on your support and teaching. When you see children concentrating, collaborating or enjoying the activities, you are doing it well. If a workshop becomes chaotic, or does not last as long as you expect, or does not go according to plan, then use this as a learning moment. Consider what you might change or prepare differently, and try again! Older children will be capable of having a discussion about boundaries, yours and theirs. Find your own style with *Understanding Through Your Hands*, and adjust and adapt as and when you think it is necessary. But, most of all, enjoy the children's 'wow' moments and their journey of creative discoveries.

IMG. 3.63   To conclude, there is a summary of the main tasks for the adult in supporting children through the creative
>   process. It may be helpful to enlarge a copy to share and discuss with the rest of the teaching team.

The basic attitude of the adult when supervising creative processes

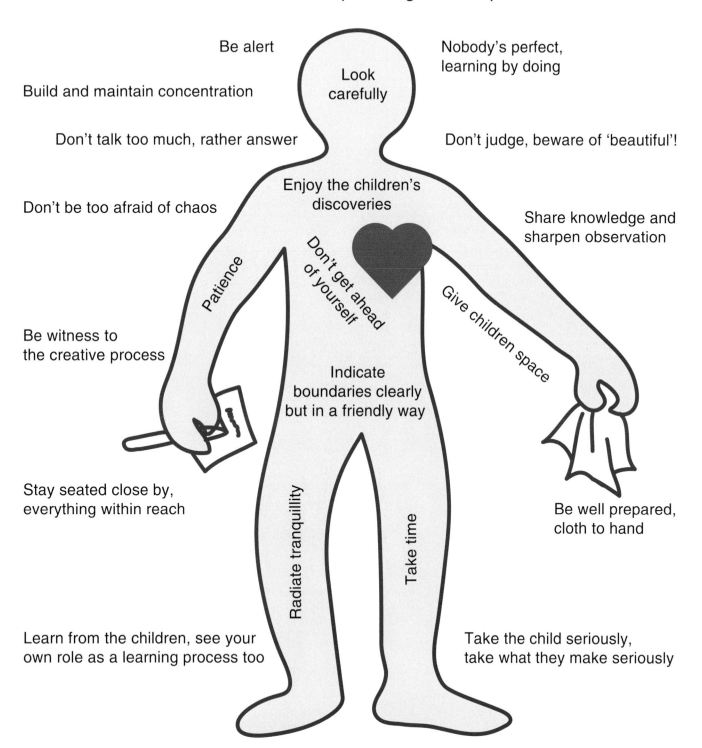

Be alert

Build and maintain concentration

Don't talk too much, rather answer

Don't be too afraid of chaos

Nobody's perfect, learning by doing

Look carefully

Don't judge, beware of 'beautiful'!

Enjoy the children's discoveries

Share knowledge and sharpen observation

Patience

Don't get ahead of yourself

Give children space

Be witness to the creative process

Indicate boundaries clearly but in a friendly way

Stay seated close by, everything within reach

Radiate tranquillity

Take time

Be well prepared, cloth to hand

Learn from the children, see your own role as a learning process too

Take the child seriously, take what they make seriously

About the authors

Sabine Plamper

Sabine Plamper is a cultural pedagogue and photographer with many years of experience, working with young children in studios. She was the artist educator at De Platanen, a Reggio Emilia-inspired children's centre in Amsterdam, in collaboration with Stichting Pedagogieontwikkeling (Pedagogy Development Foundation). She and her 'Atelier in een Koffer' colleague, Titia Sprey, have developed inspiring practical training in the field of creativity, including a two-day international course in English, and the one-year training course for Artist Educator. Since 2011, Sabine has been organising her Kris Kras Studio in Amsterdam for children starting from age 18 months. This has grown into a network of Kris Kras Studios at various locations in the Netherlands and Germany. Their work is based on a wide range of materials, without theme or assignment, as outlined in this book. See for more information about educator training courses: www.AtelierineenKoffer.nl.

Annet Weterings

Annet Weterings is an author of books and articles for childcare and primary school education. Her works include a book on experiencing nature: *Horen en zien, ruiken, voelen, proeven* (Hear and see, smell, feel, taste). She has also adapted four books by the British author Penny Tassoni on the theme of parenting, and has written a guide on promoting reading for teachers of Pedagogisch Werk and teaching assistants. Having studied pedagogy, literature and visual arts education, Annet worked as a kindergarten teacher and now facilitates workshops and training sessions for educators, teachers and lecturers.

Literature

Baeyens, J. *Het begint met kijken en luisteren. Een praktische theorie voor onderwijs aan jonge kinderen*. SWP, Amsterdam, The Netherlands, 2011.

Bakker, B., & M. Husmann. *Positief omgaan met kinderen. Praktijkboek voor ouders en andere opvoeders*. Van Gorcum, Assen, The Netherlands, 2008.

Bamford, A. *The Wow Factor: Global Research Compendium on the Impact of the Arts in Education*. Waxmann Verlag GmbH, Germany, 2006.

Bergman, V. 'Zicht op … het nieuwe leren en cultuureducatie. Achtergronden, literatuur en websites'. Cultuurnetwerk Nederland, Utrecht, The Netherlands, 2006, https://www.onderwijsmaakjesamen.nl/bijlagen/zichtopnieuweleren.pdf.

Blijswijk, R. van. 'Nederlandse onderwijskoers in Engeland en VS al op z'n retour'. In: *Trouw* (22 August 2011).

Boudry C., & H. de Weerdt. *Ontvlambare vingers. Een handleiding om te verdwalen*. SWP, Amsterdam, The Netherlands, 2008.

Breeuwsma, G. 'De vreemde zaak die opvoeden heet. Over tijgermoeders en andere fabeldieren'. In: *De psycholoog* (February 2012).

Cobra Museum voor Moderne Kunst. *Klee en Cobra. Het begint als kind*. Ludion, Antwerpen, Belgium, 2012.

Csikszentmihalyi, M. *Flow: The Psychology of Optimal Experience*. Harper Perennial Modern Classics, U.S.A., 2008.

Curtis, D., & Carter, M. *Designs for Living and Learning: Transforming Early Childhood Environments* (Second ed.). Redleaf Press, U.S.A, 2014.

Dijksterhuis, A. *Het slimme onbewuste. Denken met gevoel*. Bert Bakker, Amsterdam, The Netherlands, 2012.

Edwards, C., Gandini, L., & Forman, G. *The Hundred Languages of Children: The Reggio Emilia Approach to Early Childhood Education*. Praeger, U.S.A, 1993.

Filippini, T., & V. Vecchi. *The Wonder of Learning. The Hundred Languages of Children*. Piccinini Group, Modena, Italy, 2011.

Foks-Appelman, Th. *Kinderen geven tekens*. Eburon, Delft, The Netherlands, 2004.

Gier, A. de, & H. Postma. 'Goed vies'. In: *Volkskrant Magazine* (30 June 2012), pp. 32–36.

Goorhuis-Brouwer, S. *Alles op zijn tijd. Het jonge kind in pedagogisch perspectief*. SWP, Amsterdam, The Netherlands, 2010.

Goorhuis-Brouwer, S. *Spelenderwijs. Ontwikkeling en opvoeding van het jonge kind*. SWP, Amsterdam, The Netherlands, 2012.

Haas, S. 'Entdeckendes Lernen im Dialog. Lernwerkstätten als Orte der Selbstbildung'. In: Hammes-di Bernardo, E. (ed.): *Kompetente Erziehung zwischen Anleitung und Selbstbildung. PFV Jahresband*, Verlag das Netz, Weimar, Germany, 2007. (Article based on book.)

Hagenaars, P. 'Het beslissende boek'. In: *Cultuurplein Magazine 04* (May 2012), p. 27.

Hagenaars, P. 'Kindertekeningen, een beeldverhaal'. Introduction Exhibition Opening, 23 June 2001, Kunsthal Rotterdam, The Netherlands, 2001.

Hoekstra, M. *Een onderzoek naar de rol van de kunstenaar in Toeval Gezocht*. Praktijkonderzoek Master Kunsteducatie A.H.K, Amsterdam, The Netherlands, 2008, https://hbo-kennisbank.nl/details/sharekit_ahk:oai:surfsharekit.nl:6709e160-43ef-4287-968e-85d140f3b730?q=toeval.

Huisingh, A., R. Hulshoff Pol & E. van den Bomen. *Toeval Gezocht. Kunst, kunstenaars en jonge kinderen*. Lemniscaat, Rotterdam, the Netherlands, 2009.

Huisingh, A. Verslag symposium Toeval Gezocht, http://www.toevalgezocht.nl.

Jolles, J. *Ellis en het verbreinen. Over hersenen, gedrag & educatie*. Neuropsych Publishers, Amsterdam-Maastricht, The Netherlands, 2011.

Jolley, R. *Children & Pictures. Drawing and understanding*. Wiley-Blackwell, Oxford, U.K., 2010.

Juul, J. *Family life*, Authorhouse U.K., 2012.

Juul, J. *Your Competent Child: Toward New Basic Values for the Family*, Farrar Straus Giroux, U.S.A., 1995.

Kathke, P. *Sinn und Eigensinn des Materials. Projekte, Anregungen, Aktionen*. Vols 1 & 2, Beltz Verlag, Landsberg, Germany, 2001.

Liebau, E. 'Der Wow-Faktor. Warum künstlerische Bildung nötig ist'. In: Bamford, A. *Der Wow-Faktor. Analyse der Qualität künsterlischer Bildung*. Waxmann Verlag, Münster, Germany, 2010, pp. 11–19.

Lindsay, G. 'Do visual art experiences in early childhood settings foster educative growth or stagnation?' In: *International Art in Early Childhood Research Journal*, Vol 5, No. 1, 2016.

Meeuwig, M., W. Schepers & T. van der Werf. *SPOREN van Reggio. Introduction in de SPOREN-pedagogiek*. SWP, Amsterdam, The Netherlands, 2007.

Meulen, K. van der. 'Via kunst ontdekken kinderen de wereld'. In: *Cultuurcoördinator.nl* (January 2012), pp. 12–15.

Mieras, M. 'Kunst als slijpsteen voor het brein'. In: *Toeval Gezocht. Kunst, kunstenaars en jonge kinderen*. Lemniscaat, Rotterdam, The Netherlands, 2009, pp. 114–20.

Monden, M. 'In elk kind schuilt een kunstenaar'. In *Het Parool* (23 June 2011), https://atelierineenkoffer.nl/publicaties/.

Overduin, C. 'Een andere kijk op de wereld. Kinderen en kunst'. In: *Kinderopvang* (2007), nr. 10/11, pp. 10–18.

Plamper, S. *De waarde en de schoonheid van de krastekening*. Private publication, Amsterdam, 2011.

Plamper, S. 'Van krastekening naar eigen beeldtaal'. In: *De wereld van het jonge kind*, March 2012, https://atelierineenkoffer.nl/publicaties/.

Poll, W van de. 'Een mens is geen hersenplaatje'. In: *Trouw* (February 2011).

Ros, B. 'Kennis moet ondergeschikt zijn aan zelf ervaren'. Interview met Folkert Haanstra en Floor den Uyl. In: *Cultuurplein Magazine* (December 2011), nr. 2, pp. 8–11.

Saaltink, H. Een onderzoek naar de functie van taal tijdens het tekenen van kinderen in groep 1 en 2 van het basisonderwijs. Master Kunsteducatie AHK (2011), https://hbo-kennisbank.nl/details/sharekit_ahk:oai:surfsharekit.nl:b412f73e-c609-4ed6-8c28-99d4e8c3102d?q=%22Saaltink%2C+Hanneke%22.

Schmitter, E. 'Das Alphabet der Menschheit. Forschungen Arno Sterns über die bildliche Ursprache des Homo sapiens widersprechen der üblichen Kunstpsychologie und deuten die ersten Bilder der Frühgeschichte neu'. In: *Der Spiegel/Kultur* (2008), nr. 23.

Seitz, M. *Kinderatelier. Experimentieren, Malen, Zeichnen, Drucken und dreidimensionales Gestalten*. Kallmeyer Verlag, Seelze, Germany, 2006.

Seitz, R. *Kreative Kinder. Das Praxisbuch für Eltern und Pädagogen*. Kösel-Verlag, Müchen, Germany, 2009.

Severijnen, M. 'Leerlingen zijn geen vat dat je moet vullen, je moet een vuur in ze ontsteken'. Interview met Lodewijk Ouwens en Mark Mieras. In: *Cultuurplein Magazine* (October 2011), nr. 1, pp. 8–11.

Singer, E., & L. Kleerekoper. *Pedagogisch Kader Kindercentra 0-4 jaar*. Elsevier gezondheidszorg, Amsterdam, The Netherlands, 2009.

Stern, A. *Das Malspiel und die natürliche Spur*. Drachen Verlag Klein Jasedow, Germany, 2012.

Stern, A. *Der Malort*. Daimon Verlag, Einsiedel, Germany 2008.

Tassoni, P. et al. *Level 3 in Child Care and Education Student Book*, Pearson Education Limited, U.K. 2011.

Valck, M. de. *Aandacht voor spelen. Maak zelf het verschil*. Reed Business, Amsterdam, the Netherlands, 2012.

Valck, M. de. *Speelwijzer. Spelen kan met alles*. SWP, Amsterdam, The Netherlands, 2007.

Valck, M. de. *Wat mag…?, wat kan…? Dilemma's bij het spelen*. Elsevier gezondheidszorg, Amsterdam, The Netherlands, 2010.

Vecchi, V., & C. Giudici. *Children, Art, Artists. The Expressive Language of Children, the Artistic Language of Alberto Burri*. Reggio Children SRL, Reggio Emilia, Italy, 2008.

Vecchi, V. 'Een atelier en een kunstenaar in het kindercentrum'. In: *Kiddo* (March 2004), pp. 24–28.

Vecchi, V. *Art and Creativity in Reggio Emilia. Exploring the role and potential of ateliers in early childhood education*. Routledge, London/New York 2010.

Walder, E., & B. Zschokke B. *Sehreise. In Kindern Malfreude wecken*. Verlag Haupt, Bern, Switzerland, 2008.

Wervers, E. 'Rekenen is net zo creatief als tekenen'. Interview with Marcel van Herpen. In: *Cultuurcoördinator.nl* (January 2012) pp. 6–8.

Wilson, M., & B. Wilson. *Teaching Children to Draw*. Davis Publications Inc., U.S.A., 2009.

Our thanks go to:

All atelieristas, artist educators, visual arts teachers, art therapists, teachers, educational staff, staff, managers, executive boards, pedagogues and autodidacts who helped us during the making of this book.

Andrea Flach
Anja Booi
Ank Bredewold
Anne van Vliet
Annemieke Huisingh
Carin Hakkesteegt
Cas Alleblas
Caterina Bounailat
Claudia Zinnemers
Constance Bogers
Constance Edinger
Dagmar Arzenbacher
Dirk Drijver
Eve Rennebarth
Fatima Pirson
Gai Lindsey
Hanneke Saaltink
Heidi de Geus
Ilse van Lieshout
Ingrid Geelen-Gijsen
Ingrid Veldman
Iris Valk
Jenthe Baeyens
Jesse van der Hoogen
Kerstin Volgmann
Karen Hofmann
Karin Voogt
Lard Alleblas
Lenka Slivkova

Lilian Keck-Rudolph
Malemby Slagveer
Mare Drijver
Marc Westerberg
Mirja van der Bijl
Monique Eilertsen
Monika Bekemeier
Monique van de Peerle
Nicole Roel
Riana Homma-Jonker
Rob Martens
Rogier Alleblas
Sanne Groen
Selver Drijver
Sibylle Haas
Silke Ratzeburg
Sonja Dumont
Tanja Belder
Tanja Sap
Theo van Willigenburg
Tihana Trputec
Ursula Woerner
Vera Barink
Wilma Hendrix
Yolanda Rietbergen

With special thanks to:

Titia Sprey
Lizzie Kean
Pete Moorhouse
Annie McTavish
Lies Kromhout

Studios, children's centres, museums, shops and schools visited:

Juniorlab in de Centrale Bibliotheek Amsterdam
Atelier Turmalin, Berlin
Basisschool De Bron, Amsterdam
Basisschool De Wegwijzer, Groningen Basisschool Het Gein, Amsterdam Buitenschoolse opvang Kikonia, Max Kinderopvang, Rotterdam
INA Kindergarten Prenzlauer Berg, Berlin
Kinderdagverblijf 't Rijtuig, Max Kinderopvang, Rotterdam
Kinderdagverblijf Hestia Beethoven, Amsterdam
Kinderdagverblijf Mauritskade, Amsterdam
Kinderopvang Kiddy, KID Kindercentra, Dongen
Kindercentrum Altijd Lente, Amsterdam
Kindercentrum Mergelland, Cadier en Keer
Kindercentrum Pandaberen, Partou Kinderopvang, Amsterdam
Kindercentrum Prinses Juliana, IJsterk Kinderopvang, Amsterdam
Kindercentrum Westerdok, IJsterk Kinderopvang, Amsterdam
Kinderdagverblijf Uit de Kunst, SKA Kinderopvang, Amersfoort
Kinderdagverblijf Villa Petit Paradis, Stichting Speelwerk Meppel
Kindergarten Kinderland, Berlin
KinderKünsteZentrum, Berlin
Klax-Kindergarten, Berlin
Krinkelwinkel, 2Samen Kinderopvang, Den Haag
Kris Kras Atelier Amsterdam Oost
Kris Kras Atelier Amsterdam De Pijp
Laterna Magica, Amsterdam

Lernwerkstatt Schuppen-9, Berlin
Mal- und Lernwerkstatt van Eigenbetrieb Kindertagesstätten Nordwest, Berlin
ROC Landstede, Zwolle
Scrap XL, Rotterdam
Villa Comenius e.V., Verein für integrative Hortbetreuung, Berlin
Villa Zebra, Rotterdam

Websites

Congresses, organisations of interest:

Https://artinearlychildhood.org/
Http://www.elp.co.nz
Https://www.eecera.org
Https://www.hetjongekind.nl/

About the Reggio Emilia approach:

Https://www.reggiochildren.it/en/
Https://www.reggioalliance.org/
Https://early-education.org.uk/reggio-emilia/
Http://www.toevalgezocht.nl

Painting studios and training courses inspired by Arno Stern:

Https://www.kompetenzzentrum-malraum.de
Http://www.arnostern.com
Http://www.bettina-egger.ch
Http://www.schilderruimte.nl

Communication with children in equivalence:

Https://www.jesperjuul.net/
Https://how2talk2kids.nl
https://www.vocel.org/

Inspiration in the area of creativity:

Https://www.atelierineenkoffer.nl/
Https://www.kriskrasatelier.nl/
Https://irresistible-learning.co.uk/
https://ecartoz.com/
Http://www.abc-web.be/home/
https://rasa.be/
https://debikeytehartland.me/
Https://www.tonfeld.de

Https://www.onderzoekboek.nl/
Https://www.zoekderuimte.nl/

Tags and hashes on social media:

#understandingthroughyourhands /
#begrijpenmetjehanden
#kriskrasatelier
#atelierineenkoffer
#reggioapproach
#reggioinspired
#studioeducator / #atelierpedagoog
#thatsnotwhattheteacherhadinmind /
#zohaddejufhetnietbedacht
#selfesteem / #eigenwaarde
#markmaking / #sporenmaken
#recycle
#upcycle

Looking for inspiration
and exchange
in the creative field?

Atelier
in een koffer

Welcome in Amsterdam

2day course Understanding
Through your Hands

A mix of theory and practice,
surprising insights and many
practical new ideas.

www.atelierineenkoffer.nl/international

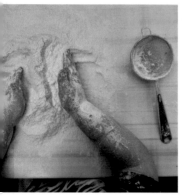

When children make beautiful drawings, we think it is wonderful. But many adults find it hard to understand what young children are doing when they scribble, smear, or draw endless lines, and why it is so difficult to motivate older children to draw or paint.

This book shows that creativity is so much more than drawing or painting something beautiful. It is a way of understanding the world through your hands and learning through art, play and science.

Drawing on the Reggio Emilia approach (among others), this book focuses on the process rather than the result and argues that children should be supported in experimenting with materials and mark-making. The authors go against traditional setups where an adult demonstrates how it should be done, showing instead that an inspiring environment and open-ended resources trigger children's intrinsic motivation. The book shows countless inexpensive possibilities, which require little preparation, and get children in a creative flow.

With its appealing full colour photographs, this fully updated English edition offers inspiration, a sustainable and feasible vision, and tools for facilitating creative processes at school, in childcare centres and at home. Full of practical guidance, it is essential reading for anyone working with children wanting to help them develop into self-aware, creative, and responsible people.

Sabine Plamper is a cultural pedagogue and photographer with many years of experience working with young children in studios. She was also the artist educator at a Reggio Emilia-inspired children's centre in Amsterdam. Since 2011, Sabine has been working with 18-month to 10-year-old children at her Kris Kras Studio and gives practical trainings for educators in the Netherlands and abroad.

Annet Weterings is an author of books and articles for childcare and primary school education. Her works include a Dutch book on experiencing nature: *Hear and see, smell, feel, taste*. She has also adapted four books by the British author Penny Tassoni on the theme of parenting and has written a guide on promoting reading for teachers and teaching assistants.

A **David Fulton** Book   EDUCATION

an **informa** business

ISBN 978-1-032-52381-1

9 781032 523811

Routledge
Taylor & Francis Group

www.routledge.com/education